# Story and Reality

# Story and Reality

*an essay on truth*

*by*

ROBERT P. ROTH

WILLIAM B. EERDMANS PUBLISHING COMPANY
Grand Rapids, Michigan

# Contents

# Part One

# AN ANALYSIS OF STORY

For centuries theology has been married to philosophy. Or better, theology has employed from time to time various philosophies as handmaidens. The type of work to be done has determined which philosophy was employed. Plato was helpful with the trinitarian formula. Aristotle was useful to convey the doctrine of the real presence of the risen Christ in the Eucharist. Idealism most clearly expressed the Christian view of the personal freedom of the human soul. But now all three of these philosophies are dead, and we cannot return to the nineteenth or eighteenth centuries or to the fourth century before Christ.

The natural thing to do, in the light of the past, is to try to express the Gospel in the prevailing philosophy of our own day. This is what Athanasius, Thomas, and Schleiermacher did in their time, and this is what Bultmann has done with existentialism, and Paul van Buren with logical empiricism in our day. Existentialism is the dominant philosophy on the continent and logical empiricism prevails in English-speaking countries. This is a valiant effort, extremely valuable in its apologetic appeal to intellectuals.

But when we study the history of this use of philosophy we find that along with its great value every one of these philosophies produces a serious error. The handmaiden begins to act as wife, the philosophy begins to give orders to the theology. Chalcedon made God a Platonic abstraction with its doctrine of the One and the Many. Thomism made the Creator an Aristotelian Cause,

9

and grace a supernatural Substance. Schleiermacher
made human feeling the locus of the perceiving of God's
otherness. Bultmann has made human decision the event
through which grace enters. Van Buren has reduced
Christology to anthropology. As valuable as these efforts
have been, they have always failed to do the job they
set out to do. We question, therefore, not this philosophy
against that one, but the use of philosophy itself as a
sufficiently valid vehicle for the Gospel.

Philosophy is not the only handmaiden employed by
theology. History has also been used. But again, in spite
of many helpful insights and much support from historians, the application of history to the Gospel ultimately
produces error, largely, no doubt, because of the use of
history as a philosophical category, but not only for this
reason. Neither the dispensationalist interpretation nor
the *Heilsgeschichte* view has done justice to the Christian
story. The category of history is simply not big enough
to contain all that is included in the biblical account,
even when the attempt is made to sanctify it by calling
it holy history. An account of how "God works in history"
is not history because it begs the question that is at stake
for the historian. God's work in history is no longer human history.

Sociology and psychology have likewise been used by
theology, but these social sciences, like history, are limited to the human. They cannot deal with those aspects
of the Gospel that do not fit human categories. Every
element which is strange to the human must either be
reduced to the human or be discarded. But we must
reckon with the fact that it is the absurd in the Christian
story that is believed, and this cannot be excised so as to
make it more believable.

In view of this disappointing survey, I suggest we look
elsewhere for help to understand and convey the Christian story. I am saying that neither philosophy nor

analytic scientific method can be the final vehicle for theological statement. Philosophy, history, sociology, psychology can all be useful and informative within the limits they set for themselves, but they can never be cross-fertilized with theology. The objection is not to a theological hanky-panky in which theology takes a mistress, but to a liaison in which philosophy becomes a nagging wife. The trouble comes when philosophical and scientific disciplines limit the Christian story to human ideas or human events or human feelings or human social organizations. The Gospel, however, is a story that is far broader. It tells a tale of many regions, many ages, many kinds of creatures — some visible, some invisible, some good, some bad, some very much mixed. It is a tall tale indeed!

Perhaps that is our clue: *tale, story*. The Gospel is not history but story. History can speak only of man's understanding of human events. The Gospel is not thought either. It is not the grandest idea either conceived by, or revealed to, man. Thought can speak only of man's understanding of the human mind. Also the Gospel is not a feeling of dependence. It is not the noblest emotion about the holy. Feeling can grasp only man's relationship with what he cherishes. Nor is the Gospel right volition. The Gospel is a happening which comes not by human decision. The Gospel is a story in which man is one character among others. His thoughts — from grand to niggardly — his feelings — from noble to mean — his actions — from courageous to cowardly — all enter into the story significantly but only alongside those of others who shape the tale. Some of these others only occasionally appear, but they are always known to be really present. Some are very strange, such as talking animals, witches, angels, and a serpent who appears as a dragon at the end.

Perhaps we had better investigate the nature of story

itself before we speak further of the Christian story. Remember we are saying that the Gospel has the character of story about it. We are not asking now if this story is true or fictional. Stories are told regardless of that question. You do not remove all dragons from stories before telling them because on prior philosophical grounds you do not believe in the existence of dragons. We are asking what it is that makes a story. Just as theology in the past studied the nature of logic and psychology and sociology so as to understand how to convey the Gospel via these vehicles, so now let us ask what is story. We are cognizant that when a species is cross-fertilized it may produce a monster, a sterile mule, or a strengthened and beautiful new species. Cross-fertilizing theology and literature to produce literary theology just possibly may not produce a monster or a mule.

Think what is involved. Literature is the expressed word of man. The Gospel is the expressed Word of God. In both we begin with the word. We are saying that the Gospel is story, that story is the nature of the very reality of which the Gospel speaks, that by story we can grasp this better than by thought or feeling or action. Not that the Gospel is only story or that story is all that the Gospel is. This would bring us to the same *cul-de-sac* we came to with philosophy, psychology, history, and sociology. But in story we have a certain character which the Gospel has which none of these others has. Moreover, I do not propose that we stop our philosophical and scientific investigations. I propose only that we recognize their limitations and in addition consider this new field.

# I

## Story as Sign

Among the many ways in which literature can be useful to theology let us consider two: (1) Literature can tell us the signs of the times, and (2) literature can carry the basic tenets of faith. First let us examine story as sign.

We can study secular art forms as we study political, economic, and social trends to discover meaning in the course of our lives. For example, current plays and novels show an interest in the existential and pragmatic and not in the supernatural. Samuel Beckett's play *Waiting for Godot* is a weird story of two miserable wretches who wait hopelessly for the coming of an absurd God who welches on his promise. The world of literature is telling us today that the seat of evil is Christianity. Evil is in the Christian view of the world, in the Christian pattern of life, in the Christian structures of society. All this began ever so respectably with Ibsen and Shaw, gained momentum with Brecht and O'Neill, and now has achieved a clarion crescendo with Ionesco and Jean Genet.

Jean-Paul Sartre tells us how the world thinks of Christian religiosity in his play *Les Mouches*, a modern twist of the old Oresteian theme. This is the story of how Argos, the city of Agamemnon, was cursed by flies sent by Zeus in punishment for the sins of a people who ac-

13

cepted the rule of Aegisthus, who had murdered Agamemnon. Aegisthus repented of his sin, however, and gave tribute to Zeus for the right to rule on Agamemnon's throne. Thus God is served by both people and monarch, and God keeps the power structure intact by using repentance to enslave the people. Orestes, the son of Agamemnon, comes to Argos to avenge his father's murder. Zeus will condone this vengeance and let Orestes sit on the throne if he will also repent and bring to Zeus the tribute of the people, but Orestes is free not to do this. Here is the modern twist. Unlike the classical hero whose tragedy was fixed by the stars, modern man knows he can be free because he is in fact free. The modern Orestes elects not to repent of his deed. He kills Aegisthus and refuses the throne, taking upon himself his own crime and not shifting it to another to bear for him. So he sets the people free from their curse and like a pied piper he leaves the city, taking the flies with him.

This, then, is a story telling us that Christian repentance enslaves us to God because as Christians we accept both his curse and the tyranny of a divinely sanctioned government. We render to God the things that are God's and to Caesar the things that are Caesar's because Caesar is ordained of God. But Sartre says we can be rid of our guilt by not paying tribute to God and by accepting the guilt as our own. Grace as forgiveness is impossible. As Shaw said: "Who wants forgiveness? A man will pay his own debt." We can be rid also of the tyranny of government when we know it is a human structure and has no absolute claims.

Albert Camus has explored this relationship between God and government, a relationship which Harvey Cox has seen so clearly in his call for the rejection of the God of metaphysics in favor of the God of the *polis*. Camus has studied the relationship in terms of man's rebellion against both God and king. In *L'Homme Revolté* he traces the history of deicide and regicide from the Marquis de Sade and the Jacobins to Nietzsche and Marx. He declares that man is essentially a rebel: "I rebel, therefore I am." But he adds: "We are alone in this world, there is no other." His rebellion begins metaphysically. Since there is no God, there is no afterlife, and we are left with historical solitude. Then we immediately ask: "If we live only to die, why exist at all? Why not suicide?"

Man the rebel, says Camus, has answered this in two ways in the past: with the absurdity of faith, and with the violence of nihilistic revolution. The absurd man of faith is Don Juan, Faust, Don Quixote, Søren Kierkegaard's Knight of Faith, any monk, or any member of Lutheran Church Women. Each in his own way has hoped in the hopeless. But such absurd faith is really not faith but wishful credulity. Truly absurd reasoning, not absurd credulity, is the lucid recognition of the limits of reasoning. Camus quotes Pindar: "O my soul, do not aspire to immortal life, but exhaust the limits of the possible." Hence he begins with the antinomies of Kant and the skepticism of Hume: One can never know reality in itself, one can never bind logic to fact. We live in a world of absurdity. It may be reasonable to reward virtue with immortal life, but there is only the absurd evidence of the lack of it.

Then again, why not despair? The second answer is the twentieth-century revolution of nihilism. This is different from previous rebellion in that it does not justify itself on principle. In the past, rebellion on principle killed God in the person of his representative on earth. The rebel in the past always appealed to a common morality with the tyrant he sought to overthrow. Unlike this moralistic rebel of the past, the nihilistic revolutionary madly exploits in order to produce a being that

we are not. He seeks to achieve dominance within history
by violently creating a new man as well as a new social
order. Only success is innocent. Only victory justifies.
Any device may be used to achieve nihilistic success —
lies, murders, deception, pogroms.

Nihilism is as abhorrent to Camus as the wishful
credulity of absurd faith. He rejects both fascism and
communism because their nihilistic materialism accepts
injustices in the present to assure justice in the historic
future. This is only a little less wishful and only a little
more humane than the Christian rebellion, which is
false because it projects hope into a transcendent future
and neglects the injustice of the present.

Since both the Christian moralistic rebellion and the
twentieth-century nihilistic revolution fail, Camus suggests we need the birth of a rebellion based on moder-
ation, a recognition of the limits of man which offers
"the only original rule of life today: to learn to live and
to die, and in order to be a man to refuse to be a god."[1]
For this reason he revives the myth of Sisyphus and
offers it as the story by which man can live and die. This
is not faith in the absurd, nor is it unprincipled revolt,
but it is acceptance of the absurd.

If Sisyphus is his mythical hero Kafka is Camus' literary hero, especially in *The Castle*, where Joseph K affirms
hope in the face of the hopeless by meeting life's defeats
with gentle patience and constant renewal. This is done
in contrast with another character in the novel, Amalia,
who has lost all hope. Kafka, says Camus, can be explained by the absurd logic of the insane. To illustrate
this logic, Camus tells the story of a man fishing in his
bathtub. With a view to therapy, the doctor attempts to
humor the man by asking, "How are they biting?" "Why
do you ask," replies the insane man, "Can't you see this

[1] *The Rebel* (London: Hamilton, 1953), p. 273.

is a bathtub?" And then he goes on fishing.[2] Kafka's
world is a strange world of absurd surprises in which a
man allows himself the tormenting luxury of fishing in
a bathtub knowing that nothing will come of it. This is
the real world, and Kafka, according to Camus, is the
best observer of it.

Oedipus gives the recipe for the absurd victory too,
says Camus. Putting his hand in the cool hand of a girl,
the blind king says: "Despite so many ordeals, my ad-
vanced age and the nobility of my soul make me conclude
all is well." So, comments Camus, "convinced of the
wholly human origin of all that is human, a blind man
eager to see knows that night has no end, he is still on
the go."[3] But Camus prefers the myth of Sisyphus to the
legend of Oedipus because it adds modern courage to
ancient wisdom. Sisyphus is the absurd hero because he
keeps up his hopeless effort rolling a rock ceaselessly to
the top of a mountain only to have it fall back of its own
weight. It is in his return to the plain to resume the
effort that Sisyphus interests Camus. Here is the moment
of consciousness when he is superior to his fate. He is
stronger than his rock. "Sisyphus teaches the higher
fidelity that negates the Gods and raises rocks."

What this amounts to is a rejection of the Christian
Gospel on the charge that Christians believe wishfully
out of a cowardly and selfishly deluded hope in personal
reward. A man will pay his own debt. A rebel who kills
to right a wrong will not repent. Repentance and forgiveness are for beggars and slaves. Man is a rebel and
he is noble and free. But his very freedom makes him
responsible. These two things, therefore, Camus declares:
the rebel man must rid himself of God and accept full
responsibility in his new freedom.

To guarantee this new freedom and realize this responsibility, man must courageously kill God. Dostoevsky

[2] *The Myth of Sisyphus* (London: Hamilton, 1942), p. 104.
[3] *Ibid.*, p. 99.

raised this question first in literature, but he did not
have the courage to kill God. Kirilov in *The Possessed*
said that in order to be truly free, absolutely independent of any tyranny on earth, a man must kill himself.
This dreadful liberty will make him independent of God
so that he can in fact take the place of God. The ultimate
tyranny is God. His place must be usurped if man is to
be free. To become God is to become free on this earth,
that is, not to serve an immortal being. For if God exists,
then all depends on him and we can do nothing against
his will. This is the frightful dependence against which
man rebels. But if he does rebel and takes his life out of
the hands of God, then he shall be God. Kirilov says
suicide is the only way to negate God and affirm one's
own liberty.

This would be foolish if it applied to everyone, but
Kirilov said that the deed was to be pedagogical and
limited to himself so that others might see that there
is freedom. Kirilov was obliged to be free, but others,
after seeing his liberation, would know that the obligation was met, and so for everyone else "All is well and
everything is permitted." One man should lay down his
life for the many. But this was not in obedience to God,
as in the Gospel, but in rebellion. This is a Calvary in
which one man rebels and all go free, instead of one man
obeying while all are obliged. The charge is made that
Christ's death did not set men free. It only made us all
obliged to worship him in abject repentance. Hence we
dwell in a city cursed with flies. We still have religion.

One flaw in Kirilov's argument is that one man cannot rebel for all. Each must be his own rebel, if this is a
human rebellion against God. Kirilov's trouble was that
he still assumed there was a God, and that he did not
have the courage to kill him. Granted that God exists,
Kirilov was right that suicide was an ultimate rebellion
against God, but not that this would liberate man. If

God exists, the dead man is just as much at God's disposal as the live man.

Therefore, as Nietzsche saw most clearly, we must not kill ourselves, but someone must kill God. This he carried out himself with dispatch, not burying the evidence nor repenting, but loudly boasting of his deed and taking full blame for it. This deicide Camus celebrates along with the painful responsibility that comes with liberation from God. Indeed all modern men of literature from Kafka to Camus accept the inference that if God no longer exists, everything depends on man. Freedom does not make us irresponsible in an absurd world. Freedom from God and his vicegerent in government makes us personally responsible to all that is good and worthy. While all is permitted, nothing must be harmed. Exploitation is the new definition of sin in the twentieth-century myth of Sisyphus. This new godless myth, with its quiet courage shorn of credulity, has become a serious rival to the Christian story, with its faith in resurrection and its ethic of sacrificial love.

In summary we have seen that literature, no less than philosophical theology, has signaled to us that modern man has lost faith in a transcendent God who promises resurrection to a new existence in heaven. In place of this wishful hope, the most sensitive writers have affirmed the natural freedom of man as a rebel who sadly accepts the hopeless absurd but yet renews himself courageously over and over again. This he does in a world in which he is alone — for there is no other, no God in the starry heavens above nor ruling behind thrones on earth; and Sisyphus is the hero, seen not in terms of the interminable punishment he bears but in terms of his courage of renewal in the face of hopeless defeat. The obvious strength in this myth is its recognition that freedom is the proper quest of man and responsibility to himself and to others is his duty.

# II

# The Nature of Story

The second use of literature is more profound and interesting to me. This is the study of story as the vehicle of reality in the Christian message. With no pretense of exhaustive treatment I offer here a few sketchy suggestions for the relevance of story to the Gospel. In most of these it will be seen how philosophy wrestles inadequately with categories which prove eminently successful in stories.

## A.  *Freedom of Action*

Just at the point where philosophy bogs down and belabors the antinomy of free will and determinism, stories come alive and jump to the complexities of life in which freedom is mixed with constraint in various degrees. No attempt is made in stories to reduce everything to a principle of sufficient reason. No attempt is made to find a necessary and sufficient cause for every effect. Stories do not yield to simplistic solutions that explain behavior patterns only in terms of environment or only in terms of heredity. Stories do not ask if the effect is less than, greater than, or equal to, the cause. Stories do not fall into these embarrassing defeats which have plagued philosophy from the beginning, because stories acknowledge the place of mystery as a natural element in reality. No attempt is made to explain mystery away or relegate it pejoratively to a realm of not-yet-discovered knowledge. Mystery is accepted as part of the real world. Free persons act out of this mystery. They act upon, and are acted upon by, their environment, which includes all the factors that touch their lives, remote and near, past and present; but none of this action reduces the mystery of freedom that gives them integrity as persons.

An example of the affirmation of freedom by story is the telling of creation in biblical and non-biblical myths alike. In *The Magician's Nephew,* C. S. Lewis has related with exciting enchantment what happened when the worlds came into being through the song of the Creator. Philosophy has tried to explain creation by means of the category of causality, making the distinction, to be sure, that Creation is First Cause. None of the Christian stories of creation use causality. Creation is by speech. Freely spoken words say: "Let there be light!" One cannot probe the mystery of speech, but one can accept it, rejoice in it, and respond to it. Here no cause determines anything, for causality inevitably purloins freedom; but creation through divine locution enriches freedom.

History is another field in which much confusion arises because of equivocation in the use of the category of causality. Some historians try to explain human events according to a logic of sufficient reason. Others seek explanation in terms of the relativities of efficient causality. But history is the free action of persons, and whenever this integrity is violated, history dies. We cannot use the term causality for the action of people upon each other and mean the same thing by it as we do when we speak of causality in a chemical equation. Stories avoid that equivocation.

## B.  *Reality and Illusion*

Both actuality and illusion are natural elements of the world in which we live, and stories recognize the many kinds of reality. Likewise in story illusion may be healthy or sick just as actuality may be good or bad. But neither is treated as a second-class category of being. Philosophy has always separated the two into different levels. Thus for Tillich reality is Being as applied to God, in contrast to existence as applied to man. Man does not have real Being. He has only an illusory becoming, and he is threatened constantly by nonbeing, which is curiously and erroneously associated with death. Reality and appearance then fall into realms of supernature and nature, with nature tending to be unreal, or at best not yet perfect. Illusion is given a pejorative sense in philosophy, just as we found to be the case with mystery; thus the world becomes pared down to manageable sequences of narrowed experience. If appearance is not considered illusory, then the reverse occurs and philosophy says that what appears is concrete and real. Universals then become relegated to abstract and unreal names. What was true of Platonic philosophy is equally true of modern empiricism. We still have two realms, nature and supernature, only a different value is placed upon them. Nature is now valued at the expense of supernature instead of the reverse. In story there is no distinction between nature and supernature, and consequently no hierarchy of values, no contempt for the illusory.

Look, for example, at the views of illusion in the current plays *Man of La Mancha* and *Who's Afraid of Virginia Woolf*. They are opposite, but in neither is illusion devaluated. In both the tension between actuality and illusion makes the play. In *La Mancha* the dream of Don Quixote lifts him to higher humanity. His illusion is his salvation, and by it he saves others. In *Virginia Woolf* Martha is sick with the illusion that she has a son. She could not have a child, yet she could not face the actuality of this disappointment and so she made up one. She tried to live a lie, and so she needed radical surgery to have her illusion excised. Both stories ring true because they recognize the reality of illusion. And illusion, like empirical fact, can be good or bad, depending upon how it is used. Stories can cope with this paradox while philosophies choke.

## C. *The Absurd*

Stories love the absurd, they feed upon it, because it too is a real part of our world. Philosophies cannot acknowledge the absurd. Some reason must be found for everything. Existentialism, to its credit, wrestles honestly with this problem, and alone among philosophies finds a place for the absurd; but existentialism, with Kierkegaard excepted, since he was not an existentialist but a teller of tales, has only accepted the absurd, never celebrated it. Stories find the absurd to be as real and enjoyable and as perversely painful as the reasonable. Take, for example, the story of "The Frog King." What could be more absurd than a frog married to a demure and lovely princess? Yet who would ever think of trying to tell this story without that absurdity just because it is not reasonable? Out of the treasure chest of the absurd in reality come the exquisite jewels of irony and humor. Without these fabulous riches man would be a poor beast.

## D. *The Progression of Time*

Stories begin once upon a time. They move through episodes to a climax and then come to an end, an end which is always open ended. Stories move. They have a

plot. And there is always room for a sequel. Life is not
a continuous hill; it is episodic like a staircase. Philosophy cannot deal with progress. Hegel's attempt to cope
with time ended in notorious failure. Only Whitehead
among the philosophers has reckoned seriously with
time, but with him time is a natural process and there
is no room for the sheer uniqueness of an event that is
*ephapax*, that happens once for all. There is really no
drama in Whitehead's sentient occasions, only adventures of ideas. The point seems to be that insofar as a
philosophy recognizes mystery, freedom, illusion, absurdity, the brokenness of time, just so far it ceases to be
a philosophy and begins to become a story. Stories deal
with many times and many realms without ever falling
into the dichotomy of the physical and the metaphysical,
the natural and the supernatural. This is as true of the
treatment of time as it is of space. Philosophy divides
space into nature and supernature, and gets into trouble
equivocating whenever it speaks of supernature spa-
tially. Theology borrowed this trouble when it tried to
speak of heaven philosophically. Philosophy likewise
divides time into the transient and the eternal, and gets
into trouble whenever it tries to speak of a timeless
eternity in temporal language. Theology again borrowed
this trouble when it tried to speak of the kingdom of
God in terms of a timeless eternity. Story deals with
many times and many realms with no division of worlds.
There is only one world, but it has many times and
places and the persons of the story pass from one to
another naturally. For example, in the Christian story
it is the nature of angels to bring messages to men.
There is nothing supernatural about angels. This nat-
uralness does not mean that their coming is without
surprise, but then that is a condition which accompanies
the coming of any free person at times.

## E. *Growth*

In story, partly because of the reality of time, there is room for change, for growth and deterioration. Characters can be edified, built up, glorified. By the same token they can be emptied, stultified, decreased. This is true for all the persons of the drama. See what this means when it is applied to both God and man in the Christian story. Man is not definable in a fixed and static nature. He has a certain integrity as the creature of God, but he is quite capable of radical change. This is not so surprising for anthropology, but when the same is said for God, we are in fairyland. God has been defined by theologians in terms of his immutable, impassible perfection with attributes of omnipotence, omniscience, and omnipresence. But the God of biblical story does not fit these categories. He is a living person who has qualities which are strange to us, which exceed anthropomorphic description, and indeed which ultimately must be simply accepted as ineffable mystery; but he comes and goes, he assumes various shapes, he acts and suffers, and insofar as he is acted upon he both diminishes and grows. In the end he leaps from glory to glory. Only Whitehead among the great philosophers has entertained the notion of a growing God, a God who in addition to his primordial nature has also a consequent nature that picks up the values that accrue in the process of nature as he snowballs through time. Such a philosophy was clearly borrowed from the Christian story, and has much to commend it except that it became pinched and narrowed when Whitehead tried to systematize the notion, thereby reducing the living person of the Gospel to an impersonal process of nature.

## F. *Conflict*

Conflict is the very stuff of which stories are made. So also with life and the world. We are carried on by the suspense. We long to know the outcome. Will it be comic or tragic or ambiguous? Will there be untempered triumph, or will triumph come through tragedy? Here the whole range of mystery, intrigue, freedom, surprise, the absurd, deception, and final solution have full play. Again philosophies have been hard put to grant this interplay of conflict. Hegel's attempt to include conflict in his system is a good example of how the most valiant efforts have failed. Hegel was bound by his logic as every philosopher is. Unlike Aristotelian deduction, which obviously cannot cope with conflict, Hegel's logic forthrightly affirms the conflict of thesis and antithesis. In purest abstraction this logic puts the thesis of Being against the antithesis of Contingency in order to produce the logical synthesis of Necessity. But a conflict is no conflict if the outcome has necessity. In the Marxist application of this logic, the Communists rest in a naive confidence in the outcome of the struggle of history. In a story, however, as truly as in history, everything could always be otherwise. This does not mean that the story does not have its own inner integrity, but that the outcome is always known to be reversible if the characters change. It is not that they cannot change; it is rather that they simply will not change. Yet sometimes they do change, as for example Pierre in Tolstoi's *War and Peace*.

## G.  *Subjection and Release*

Related to conflict is the theme of subjection and release that runs through stories. Grimm's fairy tale of "The Goose Girl" is a case in point. Here a princess was subjected to all kinds of indignities by her maid, even reduced to a goose girl while the maid took her place as the bride of a prince. But by being true to herself with gentleness and patience she is finally released and restored to her original destiny. The story of life contains pain. Some of it is evil and some of it is at best inexplicably mysterious. Some of it is brought upon us by our own mischief and some of it is inflicted upon us without cause. The problem of pain cannot be solved by philosophies that begin with dilemmas that say: "If God is God he can't be good, and if God is good he can't be God." Stories deal with evil descriptively, for evil is not an ideational opposite to the good. It is a matter of real subjection in the drama of life from which we require release.

## H. *Prohibition and Promise*

Another aspect of the drama of life that gets into stories is the progression of prohibition and promise. "Rapunzel" is the story of conflict and subjection because a prohibition was broken, but the promise of the king's son brings release in the end. A woman expecting a child longed for some rampion in a forbidden garden of an enchantress. When her husband was caught stealing the herb, he had to give his daughter to the wicked witch; but the subjection and the spell of the witch are overcome by the king's son, who in the course of his deliverance himself suffers the loss of his sight and is helped back to health at the end by the tears of his beloved Rapunzel. No philosophy can entertain such drama. The prohibition is not a code of morality that can be justified by its inherent goodness. The prohibition is simply there as a given fact of life. But the breaking of it brings pain and subjection. Yet the promise of release is given too. But this is not without pain either, and indeed the passion includes both the lover and the beloved, both the enslaved and the liberator. The close resemblance of the story of Rapunzel to the Christian story should be obvious. Here a most profound theme is carried by the simplest narration, but when theology fails to acknowledge the story aspect of reality, it produces only tedious and prolix dissertations on Law and Gospel.

## I. Desire

Desire is an element in all stories, but it is the very mother of a special kind of story, the fairy tale. The importance of desire in the human story is underscored by the fact that the whole of Oriental philosophy is dedicated to the suppression of it. J. R. R. Tolkien, who is without peer the most eminent living teller of tales, has declared in his essay "On Fairy-Stories" that, in addition to the literary values they share with other forms of literature, fairy stories in a peculiar degree offer us a fantastic escape from many things. Especially they offer us satisfaction for our oldest and deepest desire, the desire to escape from death. Moreover, the consolation of the happy ending is the true form of the fairy story. Here the happy ending performs its highest function, just as tragedy is the true function of the drama. The eucatastrophe, the sudden turn that evinces joyous consolation, says Tolkien, is the mark of the fairy story that most closely resembles the great Eucatastrophe of the Gospel.[1]

## J. Meaning

In different ages men have asked different questions about life and death, but always they have sought some basic meaning for themselves and the whole human enterprise. Ancient man grew weary of life, but he was most profoundly afraid of death; he sought a powerful God who would restore life. Medieval man was horrified by guilt, and he sought a gracious God who would set things right. Modern man has lost both hope in life and faith in righteousness, and he seeks a loving God who will bring meaningful communion in society and sensi-

[1] *Essays Presented to Charles Williams,* ed. C. S. Lewis (Grand Rapids, Mich.: Eerdmans, 1966).

tive communication between persons. Paul Tillich in
*The Courage to Be* has most clearly seen the need for
meaning in the anguished soul of modern man. We are
narrowed not only by our unforgiven guilt and our inevitable death, but especially each day by the meaningless drift of our lives. G. B. Shaw is reported to have
said that life is one damned thing after another, and
when we get old it is just buttoning and unbuttoning.
Again it is the crowning glory of story that it can restore
both faith and hope and thus provide meaning. It is the
nature of story that it carries one along with hope to the
happy ending. In story personal excitement is the meaningful part that each has to contribute to the whole,
and the great consolation is the triumphant joy in the
final outcome.

These, then, are some of the elements in story that
make it significant as a vehicle for the Christian message: freedom of action, reality and illusion, the absurd,
the progression of time, growth, conflict, subjection and
release, prohibition and promise, desire, and meaning.
Both philosophy and science prove inadequate when
they attempt to deal profoundly with these elements.
Only story can bring us vibrantly in touch with ourselves, the world, and God.

Having said all this, I am sure the persistent question
is still: Are stories true? Certainly in one sense they are
true in that they have their own inner integrity, but
that is not what really concerns people who ask this
question. People want to know if stories speak of truth
or of fiction. We may easily grant that stories speak
truly, that they carry an important and perennial truth,
but we must still determine if the things they tell about
are really true or merely imaginary? Are they hypotheti-
cal, potential, illusory? Or are they factual, concrete,
actual, real? Are there real dragons? Do they exist apart
from the story?

When we put the question this way we beg the issue, because we uncritically assume that the only reality is historical and empirical. Suppose we reject history as the ultimate court of appeal. Usually we ask if a detail in a story is historically true. Not wishing to deny the story, we honestly want to clean it up historically so as to make it more credible. Is the resurrection historically true? Was the tomb really empty? Did Peter see the risen Lord or was this report the product of a preaching event (*Sprachereignis*)? But suppose we do not ask such a question. Suppose as an experiment in thought we look at everything differently. Instead of asking how a strange and unbelievable story got mixed up in history, and then how we can get rid of it, suppose we ask how a historical detail got into the story. Suppose instead of history being final we make story the final authority.

There are great stories afoot in the world. They have a life in themselves, and from time to time historical people find their way into these stories. They contribute to the story and are in turn enriched by it. Tolkien says there is a kind of Hungarian Goulash of stories, a great cauldron of tales, stewing and steaming through the centuries. It is important to note that he says through the *centuries*, not through history, because history is only one strand in the fabric of time. There are these various stories, and portions of these stories are sometimes told among men, but the stories themselves are broader than the human elements in them, as nature for example is broader than history. People and events add to the pot and enrich its taste. So the stories grow. Examples offered by Tolkien are the mixtures of story and history in the tales of Bertha Broadfoot and King Arthur of Camelot. Bertha Broadfoot was the mother of Charlemagne, and the story that is told of her is much like that of Grimm's Goose Girl. Arthur was a historical king of dull dimensions, but he got into the Round Table legend of the Holy Grail. He both salted this soup and was salted by it. The story is bigger than the people in it, but this does not deny the historicity of either Bertha or Arthur.

I might add as an example the legend of Pink Jade, which has parallels all over the world. It is the story of a Chinese courtesan who conquered with her beauty all the kings of Asia but was bored with them all. When she was told of the King of kings, she set out on a pilgrimage to find and conquer him too, but when she found him she lost all and won everything. The story is also told in Dakar, Africa, where its heroine is the daughter of a tribal chief. It is told in the Philippines, where the heroine is an Igorot maiden. In America she is a Navaho princess. Yet this is also the Mary Magdalene story. Does this mean that Mary Magdalene was not historical? No, because you do not ask how she fits into history. You ask how her history fits into this story.[2]

You can easily see the implications for the Jesus of history. We now ask the new question: How does he fit into the Messiah story? We are not concerned to prove historical details. We would no more reject the detail of a miraculous healing than we would delete dragons or elves from fairy stories. We would recognize that some things in the story are not historical and cannot be substantiated with empirical evidence, but now we would tell the story with all its inner integrity. Finally, if it is feared that in a narrative construction of theology we will be dealing with fantasy instead of faith, my point will be missed. What is more fantastic than the Gospel itself? Once you take away its absurdity so as to make room for faith you take away precisely what it is that faith celebrates.

[2] William J. Lederer, *The Story of Pink Jade* (New York: Norton, 1966).

# III

# The Semantics of Story

Stories are made from words and sentences. These are the materials which give the story shape. What the story tells is partly determined by the shape in which it is told. An analysis of the language of story may provide a fruitful ferment for theological discussion if it is applied to the Christian story.

Confusion in communication in every area of life has forced us to stop short and examine our speech so as to discover whether we convey what we mean with clarity. More than word study is involved. There must be research into the use of both words and sentences, and then a further look into the semantics of the totality of the story.

The field of structural linguistics begins with a study of sounds as the basic units of speech. The phoneme is the atom of language. Out of these building blocks forms of words are structured. We move from phonemics to lexical morphology. But we soon discover that forms of words have different meanings in different contexts. As words are put together in sentences it is usage that determines meaning. But syntactical semantics must be distinguished from logical semantics, since words may be used with one meaning grammatically and another meaning logically. Finally usage itself must be analyzed, since it ultimately rests upon the foundational view which one happens to hold of life and the world. This last in terms of our thesis refers to the ultimate message we are trying to tell in our story. We shall see that there are many stories, and the words of each story finally receive the meaning given to them by the story itself.

We will not concern ourselves with phonemics and lexical morphology but only with the uses of words, first as images, secondly as descriptions of classes, thirdly as meaningful propositions, and fourthly as carriers of an understanding of life and the world.

## A.  *Words as Images*

Words convey thoughts or images. These images are shaped by the data given by sense impressions coupled with the selective and creative synthesis of the categories of understanding. Because of this synthesis various images are formulated, creating at once the wealth of ideas and the difficulty of sharing these ideas.

We know that there are variations of intensity and quality in the sense perceptions of different people. There are, for example, varieties of color blindness. But experience has taught us that there is enough uniformity in sense perception from person to person to allow us to fix common nouns to refer to much of our experience. Some impressions are not sensory, but they are no less real, and we have meaningful names for them. Dreams, for example, both sleeping and waking, provide basic impressions which are similar to sense impressions, although more or less distorted. The chief distinguishing characteristic is the experience of participation in the creation of this imaginary world. While the sense world is thrust upon us, and its very givenness arouses a unique impression of which we shall have to speak later, the world of dreams, even with its echoes and reflections of the sense world, is partly a world of our own making. We are, as it were, subcreators. Another basic impression is the fundamental feelings that tend to arise alongside sense impressions. The color red not only produces the impression of redness; it also suggests warmth, just as white suggests cleanness and purity. Bass sounds give the impression of slowness and solidity, while high notes bring cheer and lightness of feeling.

Impressions, however, never come to us unrelated. They are always in a context, and from this matrix come to birth new sense impressions and feeling impressions. These are partly given to us and partly produced by us. In addition to these basic impressions, we develop meaningful patterns according to our categories of understanding. We see things in relation to their quantity or quality or modality, etc. We need not review the history of philosophy from Aristotle through Kant to Whitehead on the categories of understanding. For our purposes it is sufficient to recognize that all human experience combines the givenness of impressions that are thrust upon us with the ordered patterns we make of these impressions through the subjective understanding. Subjective here does not imply a private experience. We are rather speaking of universal experiences of the mind which arise in the experiencing subject through his own exercise of his understanding. Through this exercise images are formulated, and words are the signs that point to these images. They are more or less effective as they lead the listener to the exact image in the speaker's mind.

Take, for example, the word "father." We begin with several sense impressions. A darkish, solid warmth approaches us arousing a sense of security and finality. Gradually as we grow in understanding we attach more definite meanings to the image. Not everyone has the same image, because each has his own experience both of impressions and of understanding. Apart from indi-

vidual variations within the common matrix of the father
image, there are also variations in cultures and even in
communities within cultures. Thus in ancient Hebrew
usage the father was understood to be the guardian who
demanded obedience and who provided merciful care.
The Greek image of the father was quite different. The
Greeks pictured the father as the seminal source of life.
Thus, when the term was used metaphorically to convey
the image of God as father, the two cultures developed
entirely different religious schemes and world-views.
The Hebrews retained an intensely personal view of God
and the entire creation. They did not always call God
Father, but it was certainly the personal image of father
that shaped their culture and brought it to its climax in
the event of Jesus. The Greeks, on the other hand, easily
moved from primitive presentness to an impersonal concept of the Logos as the pervasive principle of meaning
in their universe.

To begin with, both Hebrews and Greeks thought of
themselves as participants of a story. There were many
kinds of persons in the drama. Gods, angels, demons,
demi-gods, men, beasts, satyrs, departed spirits — all had
roles to play in the story. We are not at this point concerned with the various developments of their stories,
but it is necessary to note that story, and not idea or
sense impression, was the basic understanding of reality
for Greeks and Hebrews, as indeed for all other human
cultures. It is also important to recognize that the kind
of story the Greeks told lent itself later at the hands of
the philosophers to an impersonalization which inevitably reduced the story characteristics to a minimum.
Because the Greeks thought of God as seminal source
rather than personal guardian it was possible for them,
when their philosophers reflected upon their story, to
think of this source as an impersonal idea. They confused one of the analytical components of their own

experience in the story, in which they and other beings lived, with the chief character in the story. Philosophical reflection brought the insight that experience is composed of impressions and ideas, which combine to form images in the understanding. One of these ideas, for example, is the concept of perfection. This became identified with the character of the chief of the gods, and when that happened so that perfection took on the qualities of immutability and impassibility, the dramatic character of the living God receded and was gradually replaced by an idea, one of the abstractly analyzed building blocks of experience. Our thesis is that reality is the dramatic action of the story itself. Ideas and sense impressions and feeling impressions are only the elements which go together in a multitude of arrangements to give shape to stories. With our semi-Greek heritage, it is easy to mistake this movement from a personal to an impersonal view as progress in sophistication, whereas it is only a shift of imagery.

Modern man's images are blurred. To continue the same illustration, the child today does not know what to think of his father. Is he the all-American breadwinner who has abdicated his throne to his domineering wife and his tempestuous teen-aged children? Is he the pampered but fatuous and ineffectual Big Daddy of *Cat on a Hot Tin Roof*? What is the cause of this confusion? Have we lost the clear but variant views of the father held by the ancients and consequently also lost our image of God? Or is it more profoundly that we have lost our image of God and therefore have compounded our confusion about the father? Certainly the stories that are told today from Daddy Warbucks to Pappy Yokum present a different picture from the images of old. But the deepest confusion arises from the shift of attention from the *dramatis personae* to the stage properties.

Perhaps another example will help. Consider the image

of king. We are discussing words as images which ultimately become the building blocks of stories. We are
saying that different images build different stories and
that out of these stories come different cultures. Sometimes there is confusion between stories. Sometimes there
is confusion between the characters in the story and the
elements which provide material for our experience of
the story. King is an image which derives in our experience from a combination of sense impressions, feeling
impressions, and ideas of the understanding. The meaning of the king-image, however, is ultimately determined
by the story in which we find ourselves related to realities which are called kings. To the Hebrews, in the
story in which they lived, the king was the Messiah,
anointed to serve the people on behalf of God. To the
Greeks he was a despot. These different images produced
different kinds of government and legal structure. The
Israelite society was shaped by a concern for personal
obligation that stemmed from a divine imperative. Greek
and Roman culture was laid out according to a pattern
of rights. From the ancients' principle of *suum cuique*
to the property rights and the communal rights of the
moderns, we have changed the cut of the pattern but
never the cloth. We have continued the same story without changing the basic role of the character of the king.
So it has been until the modern era.

Today we are again confused, because we have no
king. The clear-cut ancient images have been lost, since
the only kings we know today are jaded symbols of fading empires or exiled playboys. A fat Farouk is hardly
a helpful image to convey the ideas of God and his
kingdom.

Not only do words like "father" and "king" change
their meanings from culture to culture, but often a single
word may simultaneously carry several images. Thus a
judge may be a critic in an architectural competition,

a magistrate, or an arbiter of a labor dispute. In communication we are not concerned with the inflexibility of the forms of words. We are interested rather in grasping the fluid meanings that pour in and out of these forms. The meanings given to words derive creatively from the combination of impressions and ideas of the understanding as these find their place in the story of human experience.

## B.  *Words as Descriptions of Classes*

It is further instructive to notice the sharp difference in the manner in which the Hebrews and the Greeks used their words. For the Greeks under the tutelage of Socrates — I suspect this was less true for Aeschylus and Homer — words were definitions. Like fences, words circumscribed with concentric circles the various species within the genus under consideration. Thus God was defined as a subject having a series of attributes. God is perfect, infinite, immutable, pure act. No limitation can be placed upon him, yet he cannot be moved nor suffer any change. For the Hebrews, on the contrary, words were descriptions. Words were used as windows, not as defining, or confining, corrals. God was conceived — or rather he was not conceived at all but acknowledged — as hidden as well as holy. Occasionally his Word would break through the veil of his hidden mystery, however, and reveal in glimpses his truth and will. Through the windows of revelation God could be seen in the image of father and king and judge, and finally he was disclosed in the person of Jesus. From this Word all words and language derive meaning. The exact meanings of these words grew out of the experience men had in the cosmic play of life, recognizing that their experiences in history and nature were sequences played out on only two of the many stages in the entire drama.

These two ways of using words, the definitive and the revelatory, produced totally different cultures. The Greeks became static while the Hebrews, through Christ, became dynamic. For the Greek there was nothing new under the sun. All is fixed by the stars. *Anangke d'oude theoi machontai.* Once the subject is established nothing new is added in the series of attributes. If an extra image is called up, it is simply a further foliation of what is originally in the subject. The whole process of communication by definition is like the Japanese paper flowers that unfold magnificently when put into water, but contain nothing that was not in them in the first place. For the Hebrew and the Christian, words provide novel suggestibility. Every new image truly magnifies the subject and adds to its glory. History never repeats itself. Because the ultimate mystery is never defined, there is the possibility for freedom, novelty, genuine surprise. The kingdom comes like a thief in the night. Since the freedom and novelty are not arbitrary, there is fervent expectation, but that which is expected brings with it the turn of joyful surprise. All cultures, therefore, and the whole process of history have a climactic aspect which provides the character of a detective story. Israel can be sent into exile and the psalmist can weep on his lyre, but yet he will sing a new song, for the Lord requires it. A remnant shall return. There is trust and hope and joy because there is no necessity. Here is another myth that makes it possible for man to carry rocks up mountains and renew himself repeatedly after frustrating defeats. Perhaps the pagan myth and the Christian story are not unrelated. Maybe we should look through the window of story for the bridges of God which will bring cultures together. Since there are similarities in the various tales that are told, perhaps they are all part of a single cosmic tale which goes beyond the dreams and imagination of any of us. But unless we can discard the deductive and definitive way of speaking when it comes to ultimate reality, we shall remain static in culture and be forever distracted by the penultimate. Deductive, definitive thinking is useful as a tool of science, but we must never mistake the tool for the goal.

The following semantic analysis may help to show how confusion in the use of words produces cultural chaos. In Greek deductive and definitive usage the sentence with subject and predicate is basic. A rational universe depends on the premise that there are things about which we can talk meaningfully, and by "meaning" we mean consistency and correspondence. Beyond this there is nothing. The world is full. There are no empty spaces. There is no mystery. On the axiom that things equal to the same things are equal to each other, exchange of predicates is easily done in this sentence-structured universe. Precisely here is the misuse of language that brought disastrous results in communication. If, for example, I say that I am eating a red, round apple, I am uttering a meaningful sentence; but if I substitute for "apple" the word "triangle," I get the nonsensical proposition: I am eating a red, round triangle. Grammatically I have broken no rules since I still have a good sentence, a subject and predicate properly related; but logically I have shifted from one class to another, and hence I have lost meaning.

In the same way we mix classes when we say the Word of God is Christ, or the Word of God is the Bible, or the Word of God is the Gospel, or the Word of God is the sermon. When we easily substitute one of these predicates for another we shatter meaning and erroneously give equal value and authority to all. Mixing verbal and logical meanings is mixing categories. Thus it becomes semantically irresponsible to give astronomical meaning to the proposition: The Son of man will come at the end of the age; or sociological meaning to the

sentence: Israel is the family of God; or political meaning to the sentence: The church is the body of Christ;
or biological meaning to the phrases: "virgin birth" and
"conceived in sin." These words have their special meaning in the story in which they are used, and we must be
careful neither to take them out of the story nor to tell
only part of the story. The theological task is the transla-
tion of words into language that is appropriate to the logic
of its claims. We must recognize that when we use the
expression "Word of God" to refer to Christ, we mean
by this narrative usage a reality more true than any object of thought or sense.

Socrates said that reality is an idea, an object of
thought; Hume said that reality is an impression, an object of the senses. Both found meaning in sentences which
could produce consistency in thought and correspondence between impressions. It has been said more than
once that all philosophy can be reduced to the two traditions of realism and nominalism. Both traditions use
Aristotelian deductive thinking with its propositional
structure, finding meaning in the right relationship between subjects and predicates.

I am not questioning merely the propositional structure of thinking as the ultimate method of deriving truth;
I am questioning also both Socratic ideas and Humean
impressions as the content of ultimate reality.

Instead of truth's being a right relationship between
subjects and predicates, as useful as this relationship
may be in many of our human endeavors, I contend that
truth is finally a right relationship between persons.
Israel, the true Israelite, is the man who has wrestled with
God. Israel is a man in a story of conflict, anguish, hope,
defeat, and victory. Israel is the man who has wrestled
with God, been defeated, but yet will not run away.
This means that neither the philosophical nor the scientific method can teach us anything about our relation-

ship with God. Our relationship to God in knowledge and being is neither propositionally determined by logical necessity nor descriptively determined by causal necessity. We can know God only when he speaks to us in a most intimate and death-dealing struggle.

Obviously, in our communication sentences are useful to provide meaning, but not all of our speaking to one another requires a sentence, and indeed not all of our communication is verbal. Some of the most significant exchanges are expressed by means of monosyllabic ejaculation. Some of the most vital meanings are transferred by way of the most common elements, such as water or bread. Other meanings come by unique and mysterious means, which can never be simulated or repeated. The one thing that all transfers of meaning have in common is the mutual experience of being involved in the story that brings the meaning to light. Propositions with subjects and predicates enter into these stories in an ancillary way, but meaning arises from the experience of personal involvement in the dramatic action.

## C.  *Words Used in Meaningful Propositions*

We have seen that sentences have a place in the story, but that meanings become confused when the limitations of propositions are not recognized or when propositions are used without regard to a proper distinction between the logical classes of their predicates. Since sentences play such an important role in communication, and since there is so much danger in the misuse of them, it is necessary for us to enter into a more precise examination of the sentence.

Once again, while recognizing the errors and limitations of every philosophy, we do not spurn the use of philosophic analysis. Perhaps our motto should be: *ou philosophia, alla philosophein.* In this connection most enlightening is the critical tradition of language analysis that has come down to us from Hume and Kant and been more recently developed by Ludwig Wittgenstein and Bertrand Russell. The logical positivists, following Hume, had said that meaning must be limited to objects of the senses. This was in contradiction to Socrates and the entire idealist tradition, which found meaning necessarily related to objects of thought. Under the early leadership of A. J. Ayer, the logical positivists formulated the Verification Principle, as they called it, to provide a criterion of meaning as a guide to truth. It stated that propositions have meaning if, and only if, sense experience is relevant to them.

Logic and mathematics do not refer to sense experience, however, and so by the criterion of the Verification Principle they are meaningless. They are valid, nevertheless, by convention, since men universally think logically. The propositions of logic and mathematics are verbal, tautological. They have no factual meaning because they talk about nothing (no sense thing); yet they are useful even if they do not belong in the same class with the descriptive statements of the sciences.

Descriptive statements are open-ended, synthetic judgments which make scientific induction possible, in contrast to the closed, analytic judgments of deductive logic. Indeed, inasmuch as descriptive statements contain genuine novelty, they have the characteristic of story, and we may make a strong case for the claim that the recognition of the reality of story brought by the Christian Gospel made it possible for modern science to bloom. At least the two enterprises, the church and science, have in common a recognition that reality is open, moving, and ripe with surprising novelty, even though this has not always been recognized by practitioners of either discipline.

Theology and ethics, however, according to the logical positivists, are both meaningless and nonconventional since they are everywhere disputed. The propositions of theology and ethics are not universally agreed upon as are the deductions from the axioms of Euclid. They are not only meaningless, but they are also useless, disruptive, and untrue.

An analysis of language therefore shows three kinds of proposition. (1) Emotive propositions declare the subjective feelings which arise in the speaker as he is related to objects of his experience. When I say this is good wine, I am not really saying anything about the wine. I am stating an emotive judgment about my feelings towards the wine. I am saying something about myself. I am really saying only that I like this wine. The same is true if I say Jesus is my Lord. I am not saying anything about Jesus except as he is held by me in my cherished possession. I am saying only that I like Jesus more than anyone else. Emotive judgments may be honest or deceptive.

(2) Verbal propositions are tautologies having universal acceptance or acquiescence. These are the propositions of mathematics and logic, which are valid or invalid according to the universal use of reason. When I say that the angles of an equilateral triangle are equal, I am not saying anything about myself or any particular triangle. I am saying something about triangularity that is accepted by definition.

(3) Descriptive propositions report factual data about objects as they are given in experience. When I say that this chalkboard is green, I am describing something outside myself which does not concern my feeling about it and which could not be known simply from the idea of a chalkboard. It might be black. Description adds synthetically to the subject. Thus we have seen that emotive statements are honest or deceiving, verbal statements are valid or invalid, descriptive statements are true or false.

These three kinds of proposition, according to the early

logical positivists, convey meaning. All others are meaningless. Confusion arises when we try to ascribe factuality to emotive or verbal propositions, or when we claim
validity for a verbalism that does not have universal
assent. Sometimes we construct sentences which have the
superficial appearance of meaningfulness but which break
down upon careful scrutiny. The statements of theology
and metaphysics fall under this criticism.

In the first place, then, propositions of subjective experience have only private meaning. They cannot legis-
late for others. But do propositions about the good have
private meaning also when we speak about good art and
good behavior and good government and the good God?
Certainly this must be said if one's aesthetics, ethics,
politics, and theology are of the type built by Schleiermacher. Within such a system of propositions one cannot say: Jesus is God. One can only say: I like Jesus.
One cannot say God exists. One can only say: I like the
the idea of an existent God. When we begin with the
notion that religion is the feeling of absolute dependence upon God, we admit from the start that dogmatic
propositions are logically ordered reflections on emotive
utterances of private religious self-consciousness.

In the second place, propositions of definition, as in
mathematics and logic, are also not testable for truth
but are valid according to the universal use of reason.
They are useful only by convention or agreement. They
have only a conventional or definitive meaning. This
agreement is not found in the verbalisms of aesthetics,
ethics, metaphysics, or theology. Hence these judgments,
we have said, are meaningless. When Aquinas, following Aristotle, defined God as *Actus Purus* he simply indulged in a meaningless tautology. Whitehead, with all
his logical erudition, followed suit when he defined God
as the concretion of being in his consequent nature.[1]

[1] *Process & Reality* (New York: Macmillan, 1941).

In the third place, propositions of fact have public meaning because they are testable. Scientific equations can be measured. Sense experience can be universally judged. The absence of such experience indicates abnormality, such as tone-deafness or hallucination. Consider the sentence: Fairies are blue. While this statement appears to be a description of fact, I soon learn, if I investigate it, that there is no evidence that anyone can muster to support me. The same evaluation must apply to statements that angels have wings or that the devil has hoofs or that God speaks. Theology cannot erect a set of descriptive propositions in the way that chemistry does. The statements of chemistry are repeatable, commensurable, and controllable. The statements of theology are not. There are, of course, many things about human behavior which we call religious that may be described with objectivity. Within this limitation contemporary empirical theologians like Paul van Buren, Ian Ramsey, and R. B. Braithwaite are attempting to work, but in the last analysis this is not theology since everything reduces to anthropology.

This critique is not new. Long before Ayer and Hume, even before Socrates, and centuries before Christ, Protagoras had said that man is the measure of all things. Yet in spite of this critique, and with full knowledge of it, sophisticated men of all cultures, as well as masses of the unsophisticated, have persistently claimed various kinds of meaning which go beyond the limitation of the Verification Principle.

Ironically it was Ludwig Wittgenstein, the foremost of the early logical positivists, who recognized that meaning goes beyond simple sense data. The modification of the Verification Principle which he proposed is that although knowledge and truth content are limited to sense data, meaning is not, because the meaning of words is determined by the use we give to the words.

According to this functional semantics, the word "good," for example, does not refer to some abstract quality that can be defined, nor does it refer to some verifiable object of empirical experience, but "good" is a word that is used in meaningful communication for the way some behavior or some objects are described or commended. This usage of commendation can be verified. Now it is possible to erect a meaningful ethics on the basis of the *de facto* use of the word "good," and this has been done with admirable success by Moritz Schlick.[2]

Furthermore it is possible to speak of religious language, because we do make meaningful distinctions between an imaginary Santa Claus, for example, and the presence of Christ in the sacrament, although in neither case can we speak of a cognitive verification of their objective existence. What do we mean when we use the expression "the risen Christ"? A group of British scholars have for the past decade addressed themselves seriously to the question of the meaning of religious language. A brief summary of the consensus to which they have come will help to lay a foundation for what we have to say about the story of the Christian faith.

R. B. Braithwaite has said that the primary question about religious statements is not whether they are true or false, but whether they can be known to be true or false.[3] The first question we must ask concerning a statement such as that a personal God created the world is how could we know it to be false. It becomes obvious that there is no way of ascertaining either the truth or falsity of such a statement, and hence we must conclude that all religious statements about a metaphysical being in relation to the natural world of our experience are unverifiable and are therefore cognitively meaningless. The

[2] *Problems of Ethics* (New York: Prentice-Hall, 1939).

[3] *An Empiricist's View of Religious Belief* (Cambridge: Cambridge University, 1955).

same is true for language about the risen Christ. We can neither prove his eucharistic presence nor disprove it. By the nature of the case this is a meaningless statement.

Braithwaite, following Wittgenstein's modification of the semantic principle in terms of function, next recognizes that although we have no cognitive information about a personal Creator or a risen Lord, we do have a use for such statements. They produce for us a guide for behavior. Because we speak of God as Creator, and because we have committed ourselves to Christ as Lord, we adhere to a certain policy of action. Not only do religious statements indicate an intention to act in a certain way, which they have in common with moral assertions, but they also tell a certain story. It is this latter distinction of Braithwaite's that is so interesting for the development of my thesis. "A religious assertion," he says, "will . . . have a propositional element which is lacking in a purely moral assertion, in that it will refer to a story as well as to an intention."[4] He recognizes that what he calls story has been called by other names as well: parable, allegory, fable, fairy tale, and myth. Story is the name I have chosen, for the same reason Braithwaite gives. It is neutral and less loaded with either metaphysical or anti-metaphysical prejudices. Also the Christian story is a comprehensive one containing shorter parables, allegories, and fables. The distinction between the Christian story and myth we shall discuss later, but the presence of history in the story is a major difference we mention in passing. It should be clear that according to Braithwaite, a Christian is one who lives "according to Christian moral principles and associates his intention with thinking of Christian stories."[5]

Paul van Buren settles for this empirical foundation established by Braithwaite, although he does not develop

---

[4] *Ibid.,* p. 24.
[5] *Ibid.,* p. 26.

the aspect of story as a vehicle for doctrine. He further-more chooses the resurrection as the starting point for the empirical experience upon which to build his secular meaning of the Gospel. Since this doctrinal construction is secular and empirical, it cannot be called a theology, if by theology we mean a word about God. It is rather an anthropology. It is strictly a word about human re-ligious experience. Van Buren builds further on the work of R. M. Hare.[6] Hare said that everyone has a funda-mental attitude which ultimately determines the course of his life. This he calls by the coined word *blik*. The Christian *blik* is the special attitude in which we find ourselves related to Jesus, the church, the Bible, other Christians, and the world. Non-Christians have another *blik*, and conversion from one *blik* to another is possible but inexplicable. *Bliks* are simply given in experience just as sense data. As the blind man at the pool of Siloam said: "Behold I was blind but now I see." We are not talking about hallucinations or wishes. When we speak of the resurrection of Jesus, we are not speaking of what may or may not have happened to Jesus, nor of wild dreams of his followers. We are speaking of observed experiences in a community that developed because of a *blik* that grasped their consciousness concerning the vitality and freedom they had received shortly after the occasion of Jesus' crucifixion.

The story that concerns van Buren is the story of Christians who have come to a new freedom through the historical incidence of the man Jesus. "Christ is risen" is the story he wants to tell; and he wants to say that this means in secular language that a new *blik* has seized a continuing community of men, a *blik* that may be de-scribed in terms of a vitality to serve others with freedom from all penultimate concerns. All other aspects of the

[6] *New Essays in Philosophical Theology,* ed. A. Flew and A. Mac-Intyre (London: SCM, 1955).

biblical record and all doctrinal elements of a cosmolog-
ical nature must be discarded because they are meaningless.

The importance van Buren gives to the resurrection
must not be denied, but neither should it be affirmed
at the expense of the incarnation, or any other aspect of
the story. It is significant that the earliest Christians and
the ensuing church tradition did not tell the story as
van Buren tells it. The earliest Christians reported that
the resurrection was a surprise to them. They did not
then claim Jesus to be Lord because he rose from the
dead. They said that he was raised from the dead because he was Lord. The resurrection was a sign along
with his miracles attesting to his Lordship. Further signs
were the miracles performed by the apostles. The story
told by the earliest Christians was about the presence
of a person who came with power. Neither the presence
nor the power had vanished in spite of the scandal of
his crucifixion, and indeed this obscene death itself had
become ironically and paradoxically a remarkable sign
of Jesus' Lordship.

Certainly the early Christians told a story about themselves and their new freedom and vitality, but they told
this only because they first proclaimed a story about
another who came to them and continued to be with
them in a mysterious presence. It is the character of this
"other" that is crucial for our understanding of the Christian story. Can we speak of him in a meaningful way,
or must we limit ourselves to speech about the *blik* that
happened to his followers? Certainly if knowledge is
defined in terms of empirical data, we must agree with
van Buren. To say more would be to say more than we
know. But the early Christians did claim to speak of the
reality of *another* in their midst. They did not claim empirical evidence, however, for the resurrection of Jesus.
They said that God allowed Jesus to appear after he rose

from the dead, not to *everyone*, but only to those witnesses whom he *chose* in advance (Acts 10:41). But
their witness was not subjective or private. They ate
and drank with him. Thus they claimed objectivity in
their experience, but admitted it was limited to a select
group.

Reports such as this from the book of Acts were not
intended to *establish* faith. If we believe because these
reports are supposedly a reliable witness of what happened, we would circumvent faith and come to religious
knowledge by the testimony of others. Ultimate authority would necessarily rest in those others who reported
to us what they know. All literal biblicism falls into this
error. But this is equally true of a dogmatic tradition
that claims a special religious knowledge that defines
its own criteria of truth. Rather what we have in the
story of Acts is a simple telling of the experience of the
disciples in all its wonder and fabled glory. That story
is not to be questioned as to whether it is true or not
true. Such a question we grant is meaningless. Some of
it is clearly history as we usually interpret and define
history; some of it is utterly fantastic and inexplicable
from the historical or any other human point of view.
Yet it is a story with the kind of integrity which any
story has, and it is a story which includes the experience
of the characters in it. This in itself is remarkable and
makes the preservation and repetition of the tale worthwhile, but the most remarkable part of the story is that
it is a serial that continues and one into which new generations of people can walk and meaningfully participate.

It would seem to be the legitimate and obligatory task
of theology to tell this story accurately, not leaving out
any of the characters or events. We should thereby stand
in the succession of St. Luke, who wrote his narratives
so as to hand down "authentic knowledge" about the

Gospel. It is understood that we can know nothing about the truth or falsity of the story itself. Theological knowledge must refer only to knowledge of what the story says. Perhaps, as I. M. Crombie believes, objective knowledge of the story itself must wait for the *Eschaton*.[7] The point is that there is an awareness which goes deeper than knowledge. Pascal said the heart has reasons the mind does not know. This is not merely wishful. There is an awareness that includes faith and hope that must also be recognized in human experience. We cannot objectively know that God is Creator or that Jesus is Lord. We can have faith that these things are objectively so and put our hopes in them. Knowledge that they are so must wait for the final Day. But in the meantime it is the task of theology to describe accurately what is the Christian belief and hope. The faith and hope of Christians is something that can be described. The sentences used in such description will not be emotive or verbal. They will be synthetic, like scientific descriptions of fact. The Christian faith is not an ideological, verbal system that can be built upon the premise that God is love. While this statement may be found on the lips of Christians, what they really are doing is telling the story that proceeds from the action that God is loving. The statement of Christian theology is the synthetic judgment that Jesus is Lord with all the surprise and novelty which this contains.

If story is the vehicle of reality rather than either thought or sensation, then recognition, not cognition, is the way we grasp reality, or are grasped by it. The characters of a story do not have knowledge of each other; they acknowledge each other in terms of some kind of response. The mystery of persons in the drama forbids mutual comprehension, but apprehension of the presence

[7] *Faith and Logic,* ed. Basil Mitchell (London: Allen and Unwin, 1957).

of another cannot be denied in the story even though there is a willful desire to ignore the other. It is this recognition, acknowledgment, apprehension — all of which is in response to another who is declared to be objectively real and not a figment of imagination nor an apparition of sick minds — that is crucial for our theological reconstruction in terms of story.

With all their commendable caution and clarity, the empirical theologians have failed to do justice to the Christian Gospel precisely because they refuse to recognize the reality of this *other*, this mysterious presence of the person who has come into human history and the story of our lives with power. This personal presence may properly be described in terms of Hare's *blik* if it is granted that the fundamental attitude comes from without by means of an encounter. It is not, however, an attitude that is formed by human decision. It is rather through the election and power of this person who from every point of view can be seen as the protagonist in the tale. But we cannot stop with the *blik*, for that would mean we reject theology for anthropology again. The *blik* is the new sight we receive because of the presence of this new person who has come into our lives.

It should be clear that all statements about such a person in the story are descriptive and synthetic even though their referent is not empirical. How then can we distinguish between statements about Jesus and statements about Buddha, green fairies, Prometheus, Santa Claus, or any other subjects whose predicates are not empirical? For an answer we must examine myth and the semantic dimension.

## D. *Words as Carriers of a World-View Story*

Several things must be said before we discuss the meaning of myth. In the first place, some statements about Jesus have historical verification. This distin-

guishes them from statements about so-called fantasy
figures like fairies or so-called mythical creatures like
Prometheus. In the second place, we must recognize the
radical shift in our thesis: We are dealing with sentences
in a story and not scientific descriptions or logical deductions. This means that the kind of distinctions we make
will not involve truth and falsity, validity or invalidity,
but rather meaningfulness and adequacy. Statements in
the Christian story need not be exclusive of statements
in a non-Christian tale. There will be differences, but it
will be more interesting to discover the bridges between
the tales by means of which the characters may interact.
The importance of this for evangelism will become clear
upon reflection. In the third place, it must be remembered that while statements about Jesus have since his
coming changed every other Christian statement, not
every statement in the Christian story is about Jesus.
There are chapters in the story both before the coming
of Jesus and apart from his coming. Yet, in spite of this
it must also be recognized that before the end, because
of the impact of Jesus upon the story, he will become a
part of every chapter. The importance of these observa-
tions will become clear as we proceed. Now let us examine the meaning of myth.

   In current theological discussion, the word "myth" is
used in a way which departs from common dictionary
definition. The dictionaries define myth as a traditional
story told to explain some phenomenon or custom. Sec-
ondarily, dictionaries often suggest that myths are necessarily fictitious. In theology, however, it is recognized
that man has looked at his world in various ways and
articulated this view in narrative forms. It seems inescapable that story is the basic key to reality. The propositions of these stories or myths cannot simply be classi-
fied as emotive, verbal, or descriptive. They are not
fictitious, nor are they empirically factual. Since men

have always developed these myths or world-view stories, we must admit a meaningfulness in their statements in addition to the honesty of desire, validity of logic, and truth of fact. The propositions of myth provide a fourth kind of statement, a statement marked by its credibility in the story by which a culture lives. Every culture, every age, has its world-view story by which it finds meaning in the mystery of life and the world. Credibility is the criterion for these statements, just as emotive statements are measured in terms of honesty, verbal statements are measured in terms of validity, and descriptive statements are measured in terms of facticity. Credibility means adequacy to meet the needs of a faith by which to live in the circumstances thrust upon a given age. The importance of meaning in such credibility statements may be seen in the fact that when the myths are no longer believed, the culture disintegrates.

We are speaking of myth as a world-view story. We must carefully distinguish between such a narrative and (1) a legend, (2) a *Weltanschauung,* and (3) a *Weltbild.*

(1) Legends arise as stories told about the heroes of history. Exaggerations and embellishments on historical data lift these heroes out of the realm of history and credit them with exploits and achievements rivaling those of the gods. Sometimes legendary accretions may appear as parts of a cosmic tale. In the realm of story there is always interpenetration between fact and fiction, actuality and illusion, history and fantasy. Legends, however, can only inspire emulation; they cannot provide credibility for a world-view. Their embellishments are therefore always subject to critical analysis according to the limitations of empirical history. Myths are not historical and must be judged on standards of adequacy to meet the needs of a culture in its progress through the story of its own life.

Although many of the stories of the Bible are legendary, and critical scholarship has the task to expose this, to treat either the entire biblical story or even the New Testament story of Jesus as a legend is to miss the fundamental character of the biblical narrative. I am not saying, in this distinction between myth and legend, that since the biblical narrative is not merely a gross historical legend, it is therefore a myth. A further distinction must be made between the biblical story and myth. Confusion arises because elements of story enter into myths, legends, history, and the unique narrative of the Bible. Sorting out all these differences in the midst of qualities which all hold in common is the task that we have set for ourselves.

The story of Peter in the New Testament, for example, is historical in origin. There may be some aspects of it which are legendary, but in the story Peter does not himself leave the realm of history, although he is reported to have had some experiences that may be interpreted as reaching beyond the limits of the historically empirical. This would apply to both the transfiguration and the resurrection experiences. In both cases, however, the story of Peter is about a man beginning in history and ending in history. With Jesus, who figures in both stories, the story is of one who comes into history from a realm beyond and who goes out of history to the realm from which he came. While Peter is purely historical and is therefore a true subject for legendary narrative, Jesus, while not unhistorical, is more than historical, more than the subject for emulation. He is, like the heroes of myths, the subject of a world-view story, but insofar as he is historical, his story differs radically in this respect, as well as in others, from myth.

Rudolf Bultmann has achieved fame in the theological world with his call for radical surgery to rid the Bible of all legendary and mythical accoutrements from both Hebrew and Greek culture. He wants to cut out everything that is not historical so that the message of the Bible may be believed. Then he attempts to express this message in the conceptual language of existentialism. His effort to separate legend from history and myth from history is laudatory. This is precisely the kind of distinction which separated canonical literature from the Gnostic Gospels in the early centuries of the Church. Without the help of scientific criticism, the early Christians accomplished much the same thing with their insistence upon a historical tie with genuine apostolic tradition.

It is furthermore correct, as Bultmann argues, that we do not commend the Gospel to faith by misplacing the offense of the message. The miracles and the resurrection, says Bultmann, are justifiably incredible to sophisticated modern man, but it is the scandal of the cross which is the Gospel's mark of distinction. This, he says, is a report which in itself is purely historical and therefore quite believable.

Bultmann also wants to avoid equivocation on the meaning of the word "believe." We do commonly equivocate with this word, but the business of theological scholarship is to avoid this and clarify the distinctions in usage. When we say we can believe history and not legendary fiction, we mean we can accept it as true in fact according to the testimony of our senses. It passes the Principle of Verification. But this belief is not the same as the belief by which we accept God as our Creator or Jesus as Lord. To reduce the Bible to the merely historical and at the same time say that its message when so reduced is justification by faith, is a flagrant case of trying to have your cake and eat it too. When we have only history we have actual facts, but these facts do not compel us to believe. Belief on the basis of facts is a natural experience we can expect of every honest person. Belief as faith in association with those facts, and not on the basis of false reports, is not natural or compelling;

it is a mysterious datum, an inexplicable, irreducible, but undeniable fact of experience alongside the facts of history and our senses. Thus while legends do not make the Gospel more believable, the historical facts in the story do not make the report in itself more compellingly believable either. Another fact is required, the fact of faith, which is mysteriously given by the election of God.

(2) Besides legend we must also distinguish *Weltanschauung* from myth. A *Weltanschauung* is a philosophical metaphor of the metaphysical structure of the world. Some philosophers have viewed the world as a cosmic idea. The Logos principle from Heraclitus through Plato and the Gnostics down to Hegel and Bradley belongs to this view. Other philosophers have viewed the world in terms of the metaphor of Substance. Aristotle and the Thomists have used this model. The metaphysical metaphor of Bergson and Whitehead is the Life Process. With such world-views the trouble is that we tend to forget they are only metaphorical and invariably are inadequate to include and explain all the facets of the world-story. Their arrogance is literalness and their error is reductionism and oversimplification. Admittedly the closest we can get to reality is through metaphors, but when a static image is used, such significant categories as time, growth, irony, and conflict are either neglected or explained away. In any case, a mythical narrative need not be committed to any metaphysical metaphor for its expression of the structure of the world.

(3) Finally myth must be distinguished from *Weltbild*. A *Weltbild* is a scientific picture of the structure of the universe. While Aristotle thought of Substance as the metaphysical basis for the world, he also thought of the world as a series of concentric spheres constructed of five elements in various combinations and motions. Today a physicist has a picture of the structure of the world derived from atomic theory. This involves the working hy-

THE SEMANTICS OF STORY

potheses of the scientific method and has nothing to do with metaphysical views of the world. Metaphors enter into scientific language too, but these metaphors do not claim to be images of ultimate reality. They are simply pictures used for convenience, constructs of the mind to help men communicate to each other about certain operations which interest them. Thus in some operations light is conceived as particles in quanta; in other operations light is more usefully measured as waves. No claim is made about the real structure of light itself. The only claim is that such metaphors are useful to solve a problem in an operation that interests scientific man.

Obviously such scientific constructs change from time to time. The *Weltbild* that was prevalent in biblical times and accepted by biblical writers was not the same as that held today, nor was it the same as that of Aristotle or Thomas Aquinas. Scientific models change according to their usefulness, and indeed there need be no single, overarching model for all scientific thinking in any given age. Many models may be entertained for different operations without contradiction. This is quite different from a *Weltanschauung,* which can never be tested functionally.

It is not true, as Bultmann assumes, that Paul held a three-story picture of the world in this scientific sense of a construct or *Weltbild.* Paul was not so naive as to think that God and the angels were literally in the sky above, and certainly he was not engaged in scientific research to discover operations by which to control the heavens above. What kind of *Weltbild* Paul did entertain we do not know. Such a model did not concern him. What did concern him was that a new power had come into the world of men in the person of Jesus, a power which released them from bondage to the elemental spirits that formerly controlled their world. Statements of this kind from Paul cannot be tested functionally by scientific method any more than a *Weltanschauung* can. They belong to the picture in the story that is told throughout the Bible. This story is neither a philosophical system nor a scientific hypothesis. It pictures a single world, the world of God's creatures. This world has many realms and many ages, and the Creator-God of them all makes his presence known in all of them: "He who descended is no other than he who ascended far above all heavens, so that he might fill the universe" (Eph. 4:10). To speak of the three-story picture of the universe in the Bible as a pre-scientific *Weltbild* is to do violence both to science and to the biblical picture.

One wonders what those scholars mean who speak of "pre-scientific" times. Perhaps they assume that along about the time of Copernicus enlightened men suddenly began to search for natural causes in their environment with the intent of gaining control over the processes of nature. Presumably, before this they merely attempted to adjust their lives in tune with the demons and spirits that controlled the universe. Theologians who speak in this fashion seem to think the world has "come of age" just recently, and this is supposed to make a difference in what we can and cannot believe.

Actually the situation was more complex in ancient times. Then too there was confusion between scientific investigation and philosophic speculation. There was also superstition then, as there is now. But prevailing religious beliefs about the gods of Mount Olympus did not prevent the ancient Greek scientists from searching for natural causes any more than a pious Christian or a devout Hindu today is hampered by his religious belief from seeking data for his chemical equations. Aristotle's physics, as well as his biology and astronomy, did not depend on his metaphysics. The accurate computation of the circumference of the earth by Eratosthenes before 200 B.C., for example, in no way depended upon current speculations concerning the auspicious ascension of the Zodiac sign of Sagittarius.

It may well be that working scientists in ancient times confused their purely scientific discipline with current astrological beliefs, but this is no different from contemporary atomic physicists failing to distinguish between the use of words in the language of science and in the language of their own living religions. Is this not a kind of schizophrenia, in which a man follows one set of rules for truth in scientific investigation and another in his religious life? No, it is simply the recognition that we use words in different contexts with different meanings. The metaphorical use of causality, we have found, is quite different in the area of science than in the story of religion. Thus a man is not asked to stop being a Christian when he becomes an atomic physicist, nor is he asked to stop being a Hindu. He most certainly is asked to stop being superstitious, however, but then a superstitious man is neither a good Christian nor a good Hindu.

What must be avoided is equivocation in the use of words. Each area of human experience has its own language. Error and confusion arise when we take meanings from one context and apply them to another without being aware of what we are doing. Man is not a compartmentalized creature, however, and inevitably he will find the different areas of his experience interpenetrating each other. It is precisely our task to find an area that is broad enough to interpenetrate every other area so that the language of that broad area may be intelligible to everyone. This is what we hope to have found in the language of story. Everyone has his story. Every human endeavor is a story. Stories are the beginning word. Stories carry us forward to an endpoint, and therefore they bring meaning without which we cannot live.

We have spoken about the stories in legends and

myths. We have described the nature of the metaphorical world-view (*Weltanschauung*) and the scientific construct (*Weltbild*). We have yet to distinguish between myths and the Christian story.

There are many kinds of myth, and it might be thought, as some have said, that the Christian story is just one of them. How does one choose between Christ and Prometheus? In form, the language about Christ and the language about Prometheus are similar. In both traditions we find the language of story. The Prometheus myth and the Christ story both have figures engaged in a plot. The plots are even similar, since Prometheus and Christ struggle with the divine, although with Prometheus there is defiance whereas with Christ there is obedience. Both suffer for their gifts to men. Prometheus is chained to a rock; Christ is nailed to a tree. Both are released from bondage and raised to positions of Lordship, although Prometheus is given only a minor place in the Olympian pantheon, while Jesus is raised to be Lord over heaven and earth.

The Prometheus myth and the Christian story were also transmitted in similar forms. Both have their origin in a community which handed them down as the tradition by which men live. They therefore set the pattern for the building of a culture. Much research has been done on the forms of religious stories, demonstrating parallels between on the one hand the Christian parables, miracle stories, apothegms, pronouncement stories, and birth stories and on the other hand similar forms in other cultures. Even the passion narrative is not unique. But there is a difference in the Christian story, where its special content gives it a form that is distinct from every other story. This difference may be seen everywhere in the story, but it is especially evident in the passion narrative. The passion of Jesus is told by eyewitnesses, yet they tell it not merely as an exercise in historical reporting, but as members of a community which has been living by a promise which has now been fulfilled in their experience. The language they use in telling the tale is therefore the language of their historic heritage, the language of the promise which they now believe to be fulfilled. The form of the passion narrative is shaped as much by the faithful hope of the Twenty-second Psalm and the prophecy of Isaiah as it is by the actual events. The witnesses knew they were living in a story, into which the history of Jesus now entered with power to bring to fruition the promise that had been made at the beginning. This gave rise to a form of telling which we call preaching or proclamation. No other religious story has this form of continuing commentary, exhortation, and teaching. The myths of mankind tell stories which come to an end. An ongoing tradition may live by them, but there is no room for growth or change in the story. They offer an explanation for human destiny, they provide a partial meaning for life, but they do not take us into a living story as actors who share in the writing of the story.

Myths are furthermore different from the Christian story in basic content. Prometheus is not rooted in remembered history. The historical actuality of Jesus is significant not because only history is real, and therefore the story about Jesus is supposedly credible, but because the historicity in the story coupled with the story in the history gives us a clue to the nature of time as an aspect of reality. Myths are timeless. The Christian story carries a people through time to a glorious climax. Meaning builds up as this community grows in the fulness of grace that is showered upon it in the presence of its Lord.

Prometheus was released from his suffering and deified. Superficially this is similar to the destiny of Jesus, but the myth of Prometheus is a story of hope in the dreams of men, while the resurrection of Jesus is a tale

of experience attested in the real presence of the risen
Lord in the sacramental life of the gathered community.
Here is a story that not only is remembered but continues to play on in the edification of the church. There
is encounter between the historical and the nonhistorical
characters in the story, an experimental meeting which
never occurs in the realm of myth. It is this encounter
with the nonhistorical, however, which gives history its
meaning in the cosmic story of Christ.

We may conclude, therefore, that the Christ story differs radically from myths both formally and substanti-
ally. Formally the Christ story has a unique preaching
tradition in which the tale is communicated with reference both to the past heritage and the future destiny of
the community in which it is told. Materially the Christian story is distinctive because of the sacramental presence of its chief character, who having been lifted up,
draws all men to himself and sends them out in service
to the world. While this presence of the risen Christ
gives meaning to both history and our personal lives, it
is this presence which also requires us to look for a category beyond history, beyond philosophical metaphors,
beyond psychological feelings, beyond sociological structures, ultimately to a category which can include all
these and yet be open ended enough to allow for the
change, growth, temporality, ambiguity, conflict, absurdity, and other mysteries which reality requires. Story
viewed as a category may possibly provide such a key to
reality if it is open enough to allow the attachment to
reality that every myth has together with its limitation.

The Prometheus myth is not to be rejected altogether,
therefore, nor are the people who lived by it. We can see
that it belongs to the Christian story in its dream and
distant hope. We can see that it is thoroughly human
in that it aspires to both freedom and power. Its profundity, adequacy, and credibility may be measured by

the degree of this aspiration as it is recognized that beyond the clash of freedom and power there is a dream of peaceful resolution. With significant modifications, the Christian story realizes this dream. The same and more may be said for all the stories of mankind in every culture and age.

Our purpose here is not to demonstrate why the Christian story is more adequate than myths, although this must be done elsewhere, but we must recognize, since myths are stories too, that there are both similarities and differences. In addition to the similarities and differences in form and content we have already noted, the origin of the Christian story has a unique quality that can be seen and acknowledged only from within the story, that is, with the eyes of faith. Whereas myths arise out of human aspiration, from the anguish of defeat and death to the hope of freedom and power, the Christian story comes as inspiration through revelation from above us, where God in Jesus comes to meet our anguish and our dream. The Christian story is not the highest and noblest story told by men in their reach for meaning and the fulfillment of their destiny. The Christian story is the surprising drama of God's reach for man in his own passionate doxology. God is not only the hero in the Christian story — it is his story in that he tells it. We do not tell it of him. He tells it through us. God himself is glorified in the telling of this story, and we enhance his glory while sharing his destiny as we enter into the suspenseful excitement of his drama.

The word that is used to refer to the reception of this inspiration and revelation is "faith." The point in human experience where history and revelation meet is faith. Since this is a unique aspect of the Christian story, we shall address ourselves to the fact and mystery of the gift of faith in the next chapter.

# IV

## History and Faith in Story

Much confusion has arisen in modern times because of our preoccupation with the historical. It is often assumed in cavalier fashion that only what can be demonstrated to be historical is real. Even nature is sometimes subsumed under the category of history, and everything nonhistorical is given a secondary rating as being merely psychological, imaginary, or hallucinatory. Theological liberals and conservatives alike get into trouble at this point. Liberals will not believe anything that cannot be proved historical, and conservatives want to prove as historical all that they believe. As a result neither recognizes the function of faith in the Christian story. For this reason it will be necessary to distinguish carefully the respective parts that history and faith have to play in the story of reality.

### A. *History in Story*

History is temporal, empirical, immanental, and meaningful. By saying that history is temporal we mean that history is comprised of a body of sequential events which are given to us in the experience of commensurable time. All history can be dated, since things happen in relation to each other in some kind of ratable sequence. These things are also empirical, in that they can be verified as sense data. They are furthermore immanental, in that they occur within the one world of space and time that is universally experienced. But in addition to these three characteristics, history has a fourth characteristic, a characteristic distinguishing it from nature, which is also temporal, empirical, and immanental. History is *meaningful*. Nature has certain categories which make it possible for us to comprehend its happenings and therefore to control them. As there are categories of understanding that are basic to all scientific investigation — space, time, relation, etc. — so there are categories of meaning that are basic to historical investigation. Huston Smith describes five such categories: trouble, hope, endeavor, trust, mystery.[1] While I might add to the categories or describe them differently, I think his thesis is both brilliant and revolutionary. Meaning, he says, may be subceptual, tacit, or articulate in the varying levels of human awareness, but it is always there and not to be denied. Comprehension of the categories of meaning will not make it possible for us to control history as we do nature, but it will help us to direct history and to accept what we cannot direct. A cautious limitation must be recognized, however, in the comprehension of meaning in history. History enters into the meaningful, but the meaningful in our lives is not limited to the historical. All history has some kind of meaning, but not all meaning is historical.

History is therefore a more or less meaningful progression of empirical events in the passage of time. History is a kind of story in actuality. It is not imagined nor dreamed. It is factual. Natural progression does not have the meaningful dialogue of story. Nature has uniformity, repeatability, controllability. History is nondirectional, nonrepeatable, unpredictable, free. History is the story of freedom and the struggle for power. Every-

[1] *Condemned to Meaning* (New York: Harper, 1965).

thing in history could be otherwise. There is genuine
novelty and surprise.

It is noteworthy that sometimes a matrix of historical
events will live on in the storied life of a community and
retain its power because of an authenticity which reaches
beyond and deeper than history. Indeed many of the
storied details which enshroud this historical matrix may
be disproved as empirical evidence but the meaning persists. Laurentius Valla, for example, disproved the Apostolic authorship of the lines of the Creed, but this has in
no way shattered the meaning of the Creed. Both its
meaning for history and its meaning in the confessional
story of the church live on. Also Form Criticism has
challenged the historical factuality of the magi in the M
tradition of the first Gospel, yet the magi live on in the
story and their meaning is recaptured generation after
generation, not least of all in our own in the beloved
television musical play *Amahl and the Night Visitors* by
Gian-Carlo Menotti.

When a story interpenetrates history, it may be told
partially as historical progression. The same story may
be told without its historical phase. The historical phase
does not necessarily make the story more real, nor does
the lack of historical phase make it less real. If a story
is real in the first place, and if this reality includes a
historical phase, we may say only that its historicity enriches the story.

The Christian story in fact has both historical and nonhistorical phases. It may be told as a historical narrative,
or it may be told in a purely mythical form, or it may
be told as a mixture of myth and history. We find in the
biblical witness to the Christian story that all three of
these forms have been used.

Mark gives us primarily a historical narrative, although
it is proclaimed in Mark that this history is part of a
larger story, namely, the story of the Son of God. Occa-

sional incidents, such as miracles, the transfiguration, and the resurrection, break out of the limits of history and attach the historical narrative to a larger meaning, but the chief concern of Mark is the historical phase of the story. The same is true of Luke, Matthew, and John. In varying degrees they present the history of Jesus, but always, and especially in John, they do so as a part of a story of the Messiah. In Matthew the history of Jesus is presented as the fulfillment of the history of the family of Abraham. In Luke the personal history of Jesus finds meaning in the context of the history of all mankind. Beginning with Adam in the genealogy of the Gospel, Luke extends his story in the book of Acts to the history of the universal missionary expansion of the church.

All these accounts emphasize the historical phase of the story, but none of them presents the history as being sufficient to carry its meaning. All point to a nonhistorical beyond which makes what happened in history real. We find just the opposite emphasis in Revelation 12 and 13, where the Messiah story is told in purely mythical form with only a slight reference to its historical phase. In a vision to the seer John, a woman appears robed with the sun, with her feet on the moon and a crown of twelve stars on her head. She is pregnant and about to be delivered of her child when a great dragon with seven heads and ten horns comes to devour the child. But the child is destined to rule all nations and is snatched up to the throne of God; the woman is also saved from the dragon. Then war breaks out in heaven, and the dragon, whose name is Satan, is cast down to earth by Michael and the angels. On earth the dragon seeks out the woman, but she is protected by God. In fury the dragon then turns his wrath to the rest of her children, to all in the church who bear witness to Jesus. Henceforth on earth there is enmity between those who follow the dragon and those who are, in the church, faithful to Jesus.

This is the Gospel without history, or almost without history, although there is reference to Jesus and the church. The form of the story is almost purely mythical, yet since the historical phase is part of the story, it cannot be left out altogether. A more balanced mixture of history and myth may be found in the early Christian hymn which Paul quotes in Philippians 2, where the mythical story of struggle in the mind of Christ is anchored in the historical resolution of this passion in the event of the cross, the kenotic death of Jesus. The story then proceeds beyond its historical phase when it proclaims the elevation of Jesus to be Lord. All creatures, historical and nonhistorical, confess his Lordship to the glory of the Father.

## B.  *Faith in Story*

We may conclude thus far that history is a meaningful kind of reality and that the Christian story embraces this reality, but that the Christian story is not merely history nor merely myth. It is a meaningful tale which has both historical and nonhistorical aspects. The authentication of history is empirical cognition. We believe what we know to be empirically given. But since the Christian story is more than historical, its authentication must arise from another criterion. The authentication of the Gospel has always been *faith*. It has been debated over the centuries whether the seat of authority for faith should reside in ecclesiastical structure, a self-authenticating book, or individual human conscience. Perhaps the solution of this quarrel lies in the direction of a balanced tension between all three, but acceptance of authority as the basis for belief is not the same as faith. Such acceptance is a natural human capacity which makes it possible for us to learn new things or join new communities or follow certain disciplines, but it does not make it possible to believe that Jesus is Lord and transform our lives in the image of Jesus' resurrected body. Grace through the Spirit must provide us with faith to do this.

Faith has often been confused with such natural capacities as cognition, emotion, volition, even sensation. Faith, to be sure, is an irreducible datum of experience, a given fact. It is not natural or universal, however, like sense data, but is given by God to his elect ones. Yet it is not private, nor esoteric, nor hallucinatory, nor visionary. Rather it is tied always to the sensory and cognitive experience of the natural man. But while it informs volition, cognition, and emotion, it is not determined by them. Knowledge, sense data, and moral decisions of the will do not make faith, but my faith shapes my understanding, my feelings, my choices.

Thus when the grace of God brings to my historical consciousness the objective events of the Christian story I apprehend them with the faith God gives me. Faith has a real object. It is not merely subjective. Nor can I produce faith by natural effort or discipline. Faith cannot be learned or conditioned. It comes by grace to all sooner or later, by the election of the Spirit. Once faith is given, it cannot be denied. It is, like the experience of a color, irreducible and inexplicable in terms of anything else. It is not to be confused with private claims of special religious visions or experiences. These may be merely hallucinations or they may be genuine, but in the latter instance they are miracles and not faith.

Luther called grace *favor dei* and faith *donum dei*. Both are given to us in God's merciful function to redeem us. Grace is the divine favor by which God works to save us and faith is the other side of the same coin by which we receive the ability to respond to this godly

passion. Grace and faith are not substantial possessions
which we can control or dispose. They are always dynamic powers which work in us both a new relation between God and us and between ourselves and others and
a new condition in our being. Faith therefore comes from
above and does not rise from within us, although it enters into our inmost being and becomes the most personal
working of the self.

How can we claim the objectivity of the datum of
faith? In the same way we infer the objectivity of the
data of the senses and of cognitive understanding.
I see a cow with my eyes and I infer there is really a
cow apart from my seeing it. Also I think cowness and
infer an object apart from my thought. I must do this to
avoid the absurdity of solipsism, but I also do it as a matter of practical experience. I have the faithful experience
of the real presence of Christ and I must infer his objectivity lest I end in metaphysical solitude, but there is
also the practical experience of every believer who shares
this compelling faith. My sight is not merely an experience of myself. My thought is not merely subjective cog-
itation in which I think about thinking. So my faith is
not wishful nor hallucinatory belief in believing.

There are thoughts corresponding to the experience of
the senses and thoughts that are free from sense images.
Faith recognizes that we are limited to sense forms in
healthy human experience, and so our experiences in
faith always have these sensory forms. Angels come to
us as men, the devil comes as a serpent, the Spirit comes
in fire, God comes as Jesus in the likeness of sinful human
flesh, the sacrament is given in the forms of bread and
wine. Yet, just as we can think of the nonsensory, we
are aware in faith of the difference between these empirical, historical forms and reality. Furthermore faith
does not grasp its object, as does cognitive experience,

but faith is given by its object. We are grasped by God in faith.

While faith is not detached from the historical, we do not limit faith to the historical, nor is the historical the thing that is believed. Both fundamentalism and neo-liberalism seek to authenticate faith by means of the historical, but faith authenticates itself. Fundamentalism says the resurrection is historical fact. The tomb was left empty because the body rose. This dangerously confuses resurrection with resuscitation, but even if that error is avoided we cannot say that faith is the credibility of historical evidence. Neo-liberalism will not believe anything that is not historical, but neither will fundamentalism. Because fundamentalists will not believe anything not historical they insist on the resurrection as historical fact. Because neo-liberals will not believe anything not historical they must "interpret" the resurrection to mean a transformation in the community due to a new freedom that was unleashed with the coming of Jesus (van Buren). Thus neither in the last analysis give room for faith, because both consider history to be all-sufficient. But faith is given by an object which is the Subject who *enters* history, that is, the person who comes from a story beyond history.

One final thing about the nature of faith should be recognized. Since faith is given, it is therefore free and does not violate the one to whom it is given but bestows upon him a new power of creativity. When God comes in grace he calls us to respond in faith. This is a creative act in which we share in the new creation. We do not cooperate in a meritorious (Pelagian) sense, but we contribute to the gracious conversation as viewer looking upon the painting of an artist, or as listener to a musical masterpiece. The artist expresses himself, communicating through his medium, but he does not say everything. He leaves something for the viewer or the listener to

say in response. Faith is a creative sharing in response
to the grace of God. In faith we add our witness to the
Word of God. We magnify the Lord as we grow in his
grace, and the witness that we return to his Word is ourselves. In this faithful witness of ourselves we contribute
creatively to the exciting story of God.

# Part Two

# THE VOICE OF GOD
# IN LITERATURE

We have analyzed story as sign and key to reality. We have found through story that reality is ambiguous, open ended, and dramatically, if mysteriously, moving toward a glorious eucatastrophe. Philosophical abstractions, whether monistic, dualistic, or pluralistic, fail to convey reality as it is experienced. We have therefore turned to story as a vehicle more suited to carry the rock of Sisyphus.

We are not saying that reality is ultimately illusory as stories are fictional. We are saying that reality is multifarious, that it includes many realms, that some are empirical and some are not, some are historical and some are not. Moreover, there is a sickness unto death that runs through all reality, whether it is historical or not, empirical or not. And against this sickness there is a holy warfare which is dedicated through suffering to bring health and wholeness to the entire creature. The nature of reality is therefore dramatic. There are persons in conflict and there is reconciliation in view. There is entrapment and slavery with the quest for freedom. There is the yearning for power and the repeated abuse of it. There is a longing for love and there are the multitudinous expressions this takes for good and evil, pain and pleasure, destruction and edification. There is the quest for holiness and the shock of exposure when the fraudulent masks of self-righteousness are torn from our faces. There is hope and the dream of release, with our pitiful waiting mocked by frustration, defeat, and death. There is the mystery that comes and goes as clouds pass over the moon. There is irony and humor, simultaneously the tragic and the comic: we find the clown face to be real because it laughs and cries at once. There is the search for meaning in the midst of a rudderless drift.

These are some of the many themes story explores. We tell their story and in the telling we are caught up in the story — not only are we moved by it, but we are also found moving with it. We will examine some aspects of only five of these themes: evil, love, holiness, hope, and meaning. Perhaps these will illustrate the thesis that reality is a story — not just a tale that is told, but a story that is really so.

# I

# A Story of Defiance and Possession

Theology has tried in various ways to define and explain evil. The ancient Greeks developed two traditions in their understanding of evil. One followed the Socratic-Platonic definition, which had its roots in Pythagorean mysticism. Socrates sought to know the good, the true, and the beautiful. He found his answer in the Delphic oracle, who told him to know himself. The truth is knowledge of what really is, and what really is is both good and beautiful. The opposite of what really is is thus false and evil and ugly. True being is good. That which does not have true being is evil. To know oneself is to know what you really are, and that is good and beautiful. Not to know oneself is ignorance and evil.

The mysticism and monism behind this view are apparent. If reality is good and rational, then nonbeing is evil and irrational. The practical significance of this view becomes manifest when the sentence is turned around, as it was most effectively in the cultural development of this premise in Oriental Buddhism and Hinduism. Evil is nonbeing. Evil is illusory. And since all experience of the senses is irrational, matter itself is considered illusory. The real is beyond the material world of the senses, and the good is escape from all sensory desire. Mystic absorption into the real being of nothingness

79

becomes the ironic exchange for the multitudinous desires after illusory things. The ideal search for *apatheia* found its practical expression in various ways, from the control of desire by the Stoics to the careless abandon to desire by the Epicureans. Both of these views were founded on the principle that final reality and ultimate goodness cannot reside in the sensual world.

The Stoics affirmed the Heraclitean principle of the Logos as the generating and sustaining reason (*logos spermatikos* and *logos endiathetos*) for all things. One must discipline himself to avoid clashing with the process of this furious reason. All evil comes from missing this mark. In personal terms, sin (*hamartia*) is defined as missing the mark, failure to know the truth and therefore missing the good that really is. Sin is ultimately a negation, an ignorance, a nothing.

The Epicureans were no less concerned to avoid the evil of this world. By inversion they reasoned that since all is illusory and transient the exploitation of the senses will make no difference. One can achieve freedom from the suffering of desire by indulging it. While the Stoics tried to deny and avoid desire, the Epicureans tried to satisfy it, but both, because of a common basic mysticism, sought to come to terms with the evil of suffering. It was taken for granted by everyone that suffering is evil, and that suffering comes by desire. The later Gnostic schools, both legalistic and antinomian, were simply historical proliferations of these earlier philosophical communities, although the Gnostic views were modified by Christian influence.

The other great tradition in ancient Greece which addressed itself to the problem of evil is the one that followed Aeschylus and Homer in regarding evil as a form of overweening pride (*hybris*) in which gods and men extend themselves beyond their appointed limitations. This, in my view, is a more adequate and profound understanding than the former, although it was the former view which became culturally determinative throughout the Orient and which has been all but dominant in the Western world until modern times. At least this is what we read in the histories of culture in both East and West, but I wonder if these histories have not been too intellectual. It would seem that another reading of the history of culture might discover a strong, if less articulate, assumption in the hearts and minds of the masses that evil is not the negation of being but rather the ambiguous conflict in which men find themselves as they live and grow and die.

Pride and the judgment of Fate upon this excess became the themes of Homer, Hesiod, Aeschylus, Sophocles, and Euripides. Here we are in the realm of story, not narrowed by discursive reason or propositional intellectualism. The themes are larger than the mind, larger than life itself. The gods seek power. The world is not their passive creature. It is a prize to be won. The resultant conflict produces pain. The Olympians wrestle with the Titans, but the conflict is not simple. A profound ambiguity enters when Prometheus defects from the side of the Titans to help the Olympians. This in itself is not the ambiguity, for it might still be thought that one side is good and the other evil, and defection from the evil side would not be reprehensible. But the situation becomes complicated when Prometheus steals fire from heaven and gives it to the race of men, who then have hope for their future and the means by which to forge tools and weapons. Evil arises from the rage of Zeus in his jealousy over the new power of men. With fire and hope men can produce a civilization which will progress to a period when one day men will have come of age and they will be able to live in the world without gods. Unleashing his wrath, Zeus curses man by sending him Pandora with her box of evils while Prometheus is nailed to a rock by Hephaestus. For thirteen generations Prometheus must remain fettered, with an eagle daily devouring his liver, until finally Heracles, a descendant of Io, sets him free by killing the eagle. Only then is Prometheus reconciled with Zeus and established in the pantheon as a god worthy to be worshipped for his gift of fire.

One cannot make a simple, airtight theological system from this story. It is a story and it remains a story. Zeus is not all powerful, nor is he all good. Prometheus has compassion and heroic courage, but he is not all good either. This is a story of conflict and reconciliation. The suffering is real and the sin is ambiguous, but the story moves to its resolution. It is a story of how suffering comes through conflict, yet the conflict is resolved with integrity. A god intervenes with compassion on behalf of men and suffers for it, but he is restored after being condemned to sink beneath the earth, and instead of releasing men from their cultic tie to the gods, as Zeus feared, Prometheus the torchbearer produces a new cult, because the children of men in the myth of Heracles worship him for his gift. If Zeus is a tyrant in the story, Prometheus is proud. Evil comes to him because of his excess. But the story does not end with *Prometheus Bound*. Aeschylus' second play finds him unbound, and all indications are that in the third play in the trilogy, which is completely lost, we would see him established in heaven as the revered Torchbearing god.

The ancient Hebrews told a different story. Evil for them was not the visitation of divine jealousy, although there was conflict in heaven and the throne of God was usurped. Satan, one of God's angels, stole not fire as a gift for men, but the whole world as a kingdom for his demonic rule. Part of this cosmic rebellion came through

the devil's coming to man in the form of a serpent and
tempting him to defy God.

God is Lord and Creator. He does not have to fight
to achieve ascendancy. He created all that there is from
nothing by the utterance of his speech. This is a metaphorical way of saying that there are two realities, one
of which depends upon the other for its existence but
neither of which can be absorbed into the other. We
have no mystic monism here. We have rather a dualism
in which the second reality is what it is by the grace of
the first, but whose integrity is never violated by the
first.

In the Hebrew story God remains inviolate, although
his creatures fall into evil. This fall does not erase the
image in which the creatures were made, nor does it
leave behind it a relic of goodness upon which to build
a restoration. The fall is total so that every facet of our
being is corrupted, yet this corrupt being is still supported by the grace of God and has not fallen into nothingness. There is nothing illusory about the evil of the
fallen creature. Nor is there any part of him which is
still good. We cannot find a good feeling which will
erase the evil thoughts and choices and actions of fallen
man. Nor can we find a good reason or a good choice.
Man has freely rebelled against God and at the same
time has become a victim of the devil. Evil in the Hebrew story involves man as both rebel and victim. He
falls from God by his own responsible defiance and by
a satanic possession which seizes him from without.
Therefore while man is personally guilty, he also belongs to a race which is universally and inextricably under demonic control. And while the corruption reaches
into every aspect of man's being, this is not to say that
he is not good. He is still God's creature, expelled from
God's garden and condemned to suffer and die, but also

the object of God's love and the recipient of God's promise of redemption.

In this story, as in the Greek myth, there is conflict
and reconciliation. The ambiguity of evil is expressed in
the way temptation ties together demonic possession
and human defiance. The Greek story also speaks of this
ambiguity, but the terms are pride and fate rather than
defiance and possession. These are not quite the same,
but the important point to remember here is that the
ambiguity of evil is recognized in both stories, and it is
recognized because the fact of evil is encountered in
story form rather than intellectually.

The Hebrews, however, did not retain their story.
Perhaps the way this should be said is that they did not
stay alive in their story. They strayed to a false god —
not of intellectualism, as did the Greeks, but of a highly
practical legalism. Evil came to be understood simplis-
tically as the breach of a moral code. There were various
degrees of this understanding, of course, and never was
the story of the garden with its profound ambiguity
completely lost, but in Pharisaism the Hebrews pushed
the notion of evil as immorality to the extreme. Thus we
find that just as the Greeks partially abandoned their
myth for an intellectual notion of evil, so the Hebrews
partially abandoned their story for a pragmatic apparatus in which the good prosper and the evil suffer, if not
in this life at least in the next.

Since ancient times, theology has given various definitions to the reality of sin. In the Middle Ages, due to the
influence of Augustine with his combination of Pauline
theology and Platonic philosophy, the notion of concupiscence was predominant. Concupiscence meant lust for
the forbidden. In its deepest sense this lust includes both
pride and defiance, because it involves not merely desire
for sensual gratification but desire to sit in the place of
God. Not only is profane love in the Platonic sense for-

bidden, but also because Paul taught that we live by grace alone all human aspiration to the divine is denied.

After the Protestant revolt and under the influence of both Puritanism and Pietism, evil came to be understood again in terms of immorality, following in the Hebrew direction of Pharisaism. If the covenant of virtue is not kept, divine punishment will follow, and again if not in this life then in the next.

The oversimplification in this view is balanced by the fact that it stresses the genuine aspect of man's personal responsibility in the evil he incurs. The irrational aspect of evil and the victimization which man suffers is neglected. As we would expect in the historical process, a phase of reaction followed this rationalistic moralism, and today we find evil described more as the sickness we suffer than the punishment we deserve. "Anxiety" is the name for sin, replacing pride, defiance, concupiscence, and immorality. An investigation of each of these constitutes the history of the doctrine of sin.

My thesis says we can learn something profound and genuine from the nature of story, and in this case we are looking for an understanding of the reality of evil. Evil is usually equated with suffering. The whole Oriental approach to evil, which derives from classical Greek views, seeks to adjust to evil through avoiding suffering by denying desire. This has also found expression in modern Western secularism, both in the popular exhortation to "keep cool" and in sophisticated techniques of psychological adjustment. The Christian view at its deepest does not minimize the evil of suffering, but by way of the cross has learned that God vanquishes evil by his own suffering and by identifying himself with our suffering.

The Christian story proclaims the incongruous irony that suffering is not evil but a way to the good. A story must start by the speaking of a word. Christianity starts with the narrative word. In the beginning the Word was spoken. This is one meaning of the prologue to the Fourth Gospel. This paraphrase avoids the inert copula and inserts instead a sinewy verb that does something. It shifts our thinking from speculative ontology to a descriptive operation. It also makes the Word passive. An action is described in which something is suffered. That which is suffered is the speaking of the Word as well as the hearing. Both speaker and hearer suffer. The speaker suffers himself to be heard and the hearer suffers the speech of the other. Thus there is suffering in creation. God speaks and he is no longer God alone, but henceforth he is both God and what he has said. He is now changed by what he has said. And we in this world are what he has said. He suffers us and is changed by us.

The speaking and suffering do not end with creation, but God continues to address himself to his people in loving compassion and long-suffering patience. Most remarkable is his voice in the story of Jesus, the man of sorrows who was acquainted with our grief. Actually the suffering of God in redemption is prior to that of creation inasmuch as God chose us in Christ "before the foundation of the world." Therefore we who are formed by God's locution receive passionately both our creaturehood and our holiness.

Meaning comes from this passion. The suffering of the Word is communication. In this passion all things find their place such that we can say amen to it, and in this trusting response we can joyfully proclaim its truth. Because God spoke in the beginning the Christian's response is ever a passionate, meaningful sermon. As Melville said:

> What could be more full of meaning? — for the pulpit is ever this earth's foremost part: all the rest comes in its rear; the pulpit leads the world. From thence it is the storm of God's quick wrath is first descried, and the bow

must bear the earliest brunt. From thence it is the God
of breezes fair or foul is first invoked for favorable winds.
Yes, the world's a ship on its passage out, and not a voyage complete; and the pulpit is its prow.[1]

Preaching, then, becomes the highly disciplined and
suffering art of communication. Indeed all forms of communication serve this passion of the Word. Painting,
music, architecture, literature, drama, dancing — all
enter into the painful labors of God. It is not just the
stammered words from the pulpit but the nonverbal
forms as well that proclaim the Lord's death until he
comes. Suffering conversation provides a view of the
world which is not static or deterministic but growing
and free. The message to be conveyed, by whatever
medium, is therefore not moralistic nor didactic but narrative. In words or color, rhythm or shape, we tell a
story. The story has excitement because it moves with
suspense. It could all be otherwise. We do not know its
conclusion, but we trust it will come out right.

We have said that stories provide a look at the signs
of the times and give us insight into the nature of reality. Our concern in this chapter is the reality of evil. First
let us look at what stories tell us about how our time
regards evil, and then let us see what stories tell us
about the reality of evil.

## A.  Story as Sign of the Meaning of Evil

We have seen in our investigation of the meaning of
evil that various cultures and periods have provided various explanations for evil. In a deeper sense, however,
all are variations on a single theme — that of the great
chain of being, as Arthur O. Lovejoy called it. From
Plato to Whitehead, thinkers have affirmed the reality
of goodness and the nonbeing of evil. In the classic view

---

[1] *Moby Dick* (New York: Heritage, 1943), p. 43.

of life there was a valiant quest for noble virtue because of a basic belief in the ultimate goodness of being.

The ancient myth said, to be sure, that fate is irrevocable. The destinies of men and nations were determined by the stars and the fixity of their periods. Adjustment was therefore the solution to life's sorrow. Even the gods had to bow to Nemesis. Tranquillity was sought through apathy, since one could not hope for joy. Peace was not victory but the cessation of struggle for gods and men. But throughout there was a basic belief in the ultimate goodness and nobility of the real.

The ancient myth found expression in the symmetry and balance of the Parthenon, in the peaceful repose of the Apollo Belvidere, in the measured cadences of Aeschylus's choruses. This old classic search for equanimity has been perpetuated to this day in the placid Buddhas and lissome Kuan Yins of Oriental otherworldliness. In the West, Christianity changed things somewhat, but for the most part the view that evil is nothing and that reality is good continued unchallenged through Augustine, Anselm, Abelard, Aquinas, Joachim of Flora, Pico della Mirandola, Kant, Hegel, and all the way down to the present. Neither the Renaissance nor the Enlightenment questioned the myth. Assurance in the face of both inexorable fate and the wrath of God rested upon the belief in a hierarchy of being with levels of reality corresponding to levels of goodness. This is the best of all possible worlds.

This common understanding of the reality of goodness and the nonbeing of evil underlay both the comic sense of life and the tragic. Laughter is evoked over the incongruous. Nothing is so ridiculous as someone's pretending to be what he is not. If he does this without seriousness, it is comical; if he does it with an earnestness upon which life depends, it is tragic. This is the humor in Hans Christian Andersen's fairy tale of the emperor's clothes. It is the tragedy of Macbeth.

In the Middle Ages evil was laughed at because it was nothing appearing as something. Artists pictured animals as men and gods to show the comedy of evil as the incongruous attempts of men and gods to be what they are not. Satyrs and fauns danced and talked and played their mischief. Forms of life on the lower levels of the hierarchy of being represented evil. The devil was pictured with the cloven hoof of a goat and a tail. Outside the cathedrals, grimacing gargoyles ironically performed the useful function of water spouts to carry away rain and evil wastes. Inside the cathedrals, carvings above the choir stalls depicted angelic figures, but beneath the seats were goblins and earth creatures of a mischievous nature. The surrealist paintings of Hieronymous Bosch with their cloacal absurdities best illustrate the Medieval view of the humor of hell.

Shakespeare expressed the Medieval view of tragedy in Macbeth, who sins by willing more than he deserved. He destroyed himself by his willful vaulting ambition which "o'erleaps itself and falls on the other side." This tragedy through the breakdown of the will is different from the ancient Greek tragedy in which the hero met his doom through the encounter of his arrogant pride with inevitable fate. Thus Oedipus kills his father and marries his mother because his destiny is fatefully fixed. Yet both expressions of tragedy say the same thing: evil is trying to be something you are not; evil is really nothing.

Against this long tradition of basic meaning, the modern world is experiencing a breakdown in meaning that is shattering our culture. Men are beginning to say to one another: Evil is not an act, neither an absurd lust to be God nor a ridiculous pride to be more than man; evil is a sickness that is suffered, a passion of pathos. So it began with the plays of Eugene O'Neill and Tennessee

Williams, and gradually the new anxiety emerged that evil is not the meaningful pretense against the reality of the good, but rather evil is not meaningful at all. Evil is something that happens to us and cannot be explained. This notion has now become the going currency in the marketplace of sophisticated ideas. It was once meaningful to say that evil ultimately originated in the false pretense of a willful person, whether this person was a god or an angel or a man. But now this meaning has been challenged, and it is considered more sophisticated to reject the myths of Prometheus and Satan and the whole hierarchy of beings and to rest simply, if uneasily, with the acceptance of the meaninglessness of evil.

There is something radically new in the contemporary challenge to the traditional system of meaning. The challenge is the nihilism of the good and the meaninglessness of evil. Take for example the treatment of death in the modern novel. For Hemingway death is a cheat, for Conrad death is a dark enigma, for Melville death is an exciting, inexorable defeat. In contrast, the old system of meaning said that death is deserved. While I have no intention of defending the traditional system, and for many reasons I welcome the new challenge because it clears the air, it should not be forgotten that it takes more courage to accept death as a just desert than to defy its meaninglessness. By the same token it also becomes possible when we courageously face death's judgment to believe in an atonement. As an enigma, death is never solved. As a defeat, it is never reversed. As a cheat, it is ever sly and deceptive. But if death is deserved, it can be pardoned, redeemed, sacrificed for, satisfied. Yet it is not within the classic system of the reality of goodness and the nonbeing of evil that death can be met either. The evil of death is not illusory nonbeing. Far from being a negation or a slipping from existence into nonbeing, death is a position and a real existence. Only the dramatic mystery of story, as we shall see later, can deal adequately with the convincing, convicting, and continuing reality of death.

This new point of view that I have called the nihilism of the good has come in modern times through the shattering skepticism of philosophers like Voltaire and Hume, who attacked the establishment with perhaps only a partial intimation of what their criticisms involved. *Ecrasez l'infame* has found its full fruition in the twentieth century, when all the rules have been broken, whether in politics, economics, morality, or art. In all fields there have been stages in the development of this point of view, and they have not always been synchronized.

One of the earlier stages in this development may be represented in the theater by the plays of Ibsen, Shaw, and Brecht. These are more than social satire. Insofar as they attack established custom, their protest may rest upon a deeper sensitivity to what is good than is generally recognized. If so, these playwrights are moralists in the traditional sense. The classical myth says that whatever is is right and whatever is is good because what is not right or not good is not. But suppose this comes to mean that whatever is is right and good because there is no difference between right and wrong, good or bad. This is what Bertold Brecht seems to be saying in *The Threepenny Opera* when he has Mack the Knife plead his final cause with a rope around his neck saying, "What is the difference between a man who robs a bank and a man who founds a bank?"

But on deeper reflection it becomes clear that Brecht is really making a social protest after all. This is a moralistic challenge thrust at a system which protects public stealing and prosecutes private stealing, a protest as old as that of the pirate who said to Alexander the

Great: "When I rob with a small ship it is piracy, but when you come with a fleet it is the heroism of empire." But even if we recognize that Brecht's socialism is still resting on traditional morality, we must also admit that his protest is so bitter and so universally directed at every convention that there is nothing left that can be called good. It is this absolute bitterness that foreshadows the new nihilism.

Another stage in the development of this new point of view may be represented by plays such as *West Side Story,* which enjoy general popularity because of their honest realism. Here the playwright utters a prophetic cry, but it is a wail only, with no promise. It is the lack of promise in the prophecy that portends the new nihilism. The tragic theme is carried in the play with grace and dignity, relieved only sparingly in a light scene of analysis in which the hoods in one of the rival gangs examine their own problem according to the counsel first of the sociologists and then of the psychologists. It is concluded that they have a "social disease," but they cannot go home to their parents for cure because parents would be a bad influence. The gentle ridicule of this analysis is evidently prompted by the ridiculousness of the methods of sociologists and psychologists, who, according to the play, only name names and solve no riddles.

This scene is followed by action charged with tense, heavy emotion, in which the law comes in to break up the mounting tension between the gangs. The law is treated with more seriousness because it is what we must reckon with seriously, but it is also treated with bitter irony because of its failure. Here the law is not represented as blindfolded justice fairly executing prescriptions for civil righteousness, but it is pictured as biased, ambitious politics aiming for promotion through favor and privilege.

The cross in the background gives us the symbol of religion. The family altar and the dance hall with gothic windows give us the place of religion. And Maria's hasty prayer in time of trouble gives us the habit of religion. But there is no priest, no mass, no suggestion of the possibility of the function of the sacrament. The most bitter line of the play comes when Doc in the candy shop asks the boys when they will stop making the world such a mess, and one of them says, "Listen, Doc, we did not make this world!"

This is bitter denunciation with no promise of redemption. The playwright gives us law without gospel. But there is still meaning, if only in the flies, for there is the unmistakable statement that what has happened is wrong, that it should have been otherwise even if it could not have been so. This much the modern play retains of the formal structure of *Romeo and Juliet,* from which it was modeled.

A final step in the modern breakdown of meaning has been made by the avant-garde authors of the so-called Theater of the Absurd. In addition to bitter protest and withering honesty, authors like Jean Genet, Harold Pinter, and Samuel Beckett have contributed cynical despair. The absurd has often been used in every art form to provide intriguing ambiguity against an ultimate backdrop of meaning. As William Kerr has said: "The degree to which a play is ambiguous but knowable in and through its ambiguity, is often the measure of our affection and respect for it."[2] But the absurd presented by Samuel Beckett in *Endgame,* for example, is of a different kind. It is not played against a basic core of absolutes. The purpose of the absurd is not to clarify the absolute but to assert vapid pointlessness. This is the new thing that hovers over our culture, the cynical de-

[2] "Making a Cult of Confusion," *Horizon,* September, 1962, p. 34.

spair of meaninglessness that has broken the great chain of being.

In *Endgame* Beckett proclaims the pointlessness of life by probing the interior of a man's heart, mind and soul as he deteriorates in the last stages of his death agony. There are four actors on the stage. They are not characters in a drama. They do not play roles of protagonist and antagonist in the development of a plot. There is tension between them, but nothing really happens. There are no events, yet the play does move to a climax. The play may be interpreted on several levels, and the measure of its greatness is that it cannot be exhaustively understood on any one of these levels. Thus it may be a drama of one man's death, or it may be a Jungian analysis of the psychology of the race, or it may have universal eschatological overtones. On any level, however, it describes the deterioration of life into nothingness.

One of the actors, Hamm, is blind and bound to a wheelchair. Another, Clov, is bound to Hamm as his servant. Hamm is sensual, domineering, self-indulgent, untidy. Clov is rational, submissive, servile, orderly. They depend upon each other as the heart and the mind in a complete personality. The stage is a bare room with two small windows on opposite walls looking like eyes out to the land on one side and the sea on the other; but nothing happens out there — even the tides have stopped. On one side of the room are two ashcans from which occasionally two old people pop up and down. They are Hamm's parents or his fading memory. In any case they are discarded like trash, and only occasionally do they intrude to nag and remind us of the guilt of the past. The climax, if this is what it can be called, is when Clov looks through the window and sees a small boy coming. Now, Hamm says, it is the end. Throughout the play the tension has built over the need of Hamm and

Clov for each other. But with the coming of the small boy, Hamm says Clov can go. If he goes it will mean that he kills Hamm, for Hamm needs his service to live, and also that Clov will commit suicide, for Hamm has the only source of food. But now he can go. This is because Clov sees the boy sitting on his haunches contemplating his navel. The boy does not come. He does not move. He does nothing. But Clov now sees him in this posture, and it is the symbol of mystic meditation. Beckett seems to be saying that the only release we can find for the tension between the heart and mind in the dying soul is when the mind sees what the heart knows — the despair that the only reality is the reality of nothing. When you can turn away from all things — memories of the past, hopes of the future, sensualities of the present — and direct your gaze inwardly into nothingness, then there is peace.

The sign of new challenge in our time which the Theater of the Absurd brings is the nihilism of the good. Ancient and Medieval man said that there is goodness and it is real. Evil is the absence of goodness as dark is the absence of light. Evil is therefore nothing, but good is something. But modern man is saying there is no light or dark, no evil or good. The pain of the world is ultimate and irredeemable. All is vanity. Really vanity. Not as the preacher in Ecclesiastes said against the abiding goodness and truth in God, but all is nothing against nothing.

Is this all that can be said? Must we choose between these two myths, the classical myth that goodness is real and evil is nothing, and the modern myth of nihilism? No, it is far worse and far better. There are other possibilities. We can say that evil is something against the backdrop of good that is also something, the something that suffers the real evil that is and triumphs over it. This is the really new word that must be said. It is, of

course, an old story, but it is always new, as the history
of thought and events and art demonstrates. Evil is not
just something that can be laughed at. This is a rational,
meaningful view, but it is a wrong reason. Evil is a position. It is not merely pride, nor lust, nor the pathetic
absurd. These too can be laughed at, not with laughter
trusting in the victory of goodness, but with the hollow
laughter of cynicism. But evil is the horror of rebellion
against a person. It cannot be defined in anthropological
or psychological terms, but only in theological terms.
We must say: Because there is Another, rebellion against
him is real and positive. Evil is both something and
meaningful because good is both something and meaningful.

There is communication in a world in which evil is
something and good is something. There is story — real
struggle, climax, and conclusion. There is no timeless
nothing, no retreat from the illusoriness of the material
world. There is rather the suffering affirmation of the
victory of God in his material world. This is the message
of the Word, the message of suffering action and active
passion. The world is the story of the spoken word,
spoken and heard and answered with both yes and no,
and with continued conversation that conquers the no
and edifies the yes. The conversation goes beyond the
language of logic and logic's precision in science and
philosophy. Truth is greater than the word of language
as God is greater than the Word of the Trinity, though
the Word is all God and not less than divine. So the
word of language may be all true and not less than true,
but yet beyond the word is the mystery of nonverbal
truth which yet may be known and communicated. Because of this, art is both possible and necessary. And we
must be particularly thankful to art in the Theater of
the Absurd for calling this to our attention. But art must
also communicate the meaningful truth that suffering

serves to conquer all violence and evil and death. This is the position which gives evil its due as well as good, and ends with the laughter of joy.

The revolutionary novelty of our time is not just a shift in interest from ontology to epistemology, from metaphysics to controllable operations, from ghosts in the machine to the machine, from laissez-faire politico-economics to socialism. These pragmatic concerns are characteristic of our age; but when we say that evil is no longer defined as nonbeing but as meaningless, we are speaking of a radical revolution, we are shifting myths. A new way of looking at life and the world is involved. Man has come to a new cynicism, a nihilistic understanding of himself which is a threat to his very existence.

The Christian challenge, however, strikes at both the classical myth about being and the modern myth about meaning. The Christian view gives meaning to being and being to meaning. The modern protest against the rational meaning of the great chain is justified, and it is interesting that this protest comes first and most explicitly from artists; but it is too easy just to assert meaninglessness and let it go at that. Especially is it too easy if this is done out of fatigue and despair because a traditional form of meaning has been found inadequate. One must move on with maturity from the position of doubt to a higher understanding of meaning. Because God has become man in Jesus, man sees himself to be neither the devil's dupe nor God's grim joke, but the beloved creature of God's suffering love. This meaning is the holy humor that sings through sadness as God calls to God: "Why hast thou forsaken me?"

## B.  *Story as Key to the Reality of Evil*

More significant than a sign-of-our-time, story is the

key to the reality of evil. We found that evil was defined and explained at various times and in various cultures as excessive pride (*hybris*), missing the mark through ignorance (*hamartia*), defiant rebellion (*hattath*), lust (*concupiscentia*), immorality, and anxiety (*Angst*). In story we find characters who manifest all these sins, all of which have the mark of personal responsibility; but in addition we find in every living story that is told an aspect of overpowering necessity in the evil that occurs. Where evil appears, each character involved contributes to the pain through his personal rebellion, and also each character is an unfortunate victim of the evil that is thrust upon him. There is both defiance and demonic possession, and these are tied together by temptation.

Because we are both rebels and victims there is an ambiguity in guilt. All the great stories in literature reveal this ambiguity. We have already seen it to be the case in our review of the stories of Prometheus and Adam. In some stories the rebel motif is dominant, and in others the victim motif is stressed. Perhaps each age needs its peculiar emphasis, but the greatest stories, those which live for every age, give proper attention to both themes.

Shakespeare's *Hamlet* has perennial meaning because the tragedy embraces the human situation in its total pathos. We can sympathize with Hamlet because we know he is a victim of overwhelming circumstances, as we are overwhelmed, and we know also that he was personally guilty, as we are guilty. Moreover, the tragedy is real because it all could have been otherwise. In this respect *Hamlet* is sharply contrasted to the modern plays of absurdity. Beckett's *Endgame* is not a tragedy. The question as to whether it could have come out otherwise is meaningless because no action takes place, no plot occurs, nothing comes out at all. Perhaps it may be called a comedy since it does evoke hilarious laughter, but the incongruity calls forth the hollow laughter of cynicism since we find ourselves laughing at our false pretense at meaning in a life which has no meaning. There is sympathy, even tenderness, in the absurd plays, since they picture the pathos of the human situation, and we cannot help crying for ourselves. But if we listen carefully, we must hear the playwright mocking our tears.

It is quite the opposite with *Hamlet*. Here the playwright celebrates the tragedy because he believes it could have and should have been avoided. Life is real, and in the story of life tragedy comes because circumstances congeal and we react to these situations with stupidity, arrogance, greed, defiance, and all the rest of the host of sinful responses which reside deep in the hearts of us all. Most of all, the tragedy of *Hamlet* reveals the utter senselessness of our actions as they are seen after the fact. Before, they seemed so freely willed and so rationally conceived.

Hamlet is a young prince hastily called home from college because his father, the king of Denmark, has been killed. Hamlet is convinced that his uncle, the new king, who has too quickly taken Hamlet's mother as his queen, is guilty of his father's murder. When the prince is upbraided by his mother for suspecting his uncle, he turns on her with a fury of denunciation. So violent is he that she cries out in sudden alarm, and her cry is echoed by someone hiding in the curtains nearby. Hamlet, thinking it to be his uncle, runs his rapier through the cloth and kills Polonius, the father of Hamlet's beloved Ophelia, who was rather innocently eavesdropping. The tangled web has now been spun, and the mounting tragedy that follows upon this senseless death has already been established in the pattern.

Claudius, the uncle, has willfully seized the throne through murder. This evil is thrust upon Hamlet, who reacts to it with maddened violence. The madness in the play is not only the mental collapse of the fragile Ophelia, nor the feigned madness of Hamlet; it is more profoundly the demonic possession which seizes the characters one after the other as the tragic circumstances are thrust upon them and as they freely and defiantly enter into the tempting trap of successive events.

Most of Shakespeare's plays, however, and also those of Molière, Marlowe, and Ben Jonson, emphasize the rebel theme as the reason for evil and the source of tragedy, to the neglect of the victim motif. Certainly this is true of Molière's Don Juan, whose downfall is due to his willful defiance against the divine. Don Juan's greatest pleasure is to trick women and leave them dishonored, but he does this ultimately as a gesture of rebellion against God, freely choosing to break the law and take hell rather than knuckle under divine sovereignty. At first in the literary history of the Don Juan theme, in Tirso de Molina's play *The Trickster of Seville and the Guest of Stone,* Don Juan is a genuine villain deserving his death and condemnation because he has dared to defy the supernatural. Later, already suggested in the treatment of Molière, because the age of reason began to doubt the absoluteness of the supernatural, Don Juan becomes more of a hero, and while his defiance is still tragic, it becomes celebrated. The ambiguity of his tragic evil is like that of Prometheus. It is true that what he does is wrong, and he must pay for it, but the tyranny of heaven must also be defied, and hence there is no escape from the tragedy.

But perhaps the best illustration of willful defiance is in Shakespeare's *Richard III.* Here we find history told in story form closer to reality than historians ever dreamed. Richard is base in his unalloyed greed for power. He will stop at nothing in his nefarious scheming to seize the throne of England. He interrupts the funeral procession of the king, whose murder he committed, and with the consummate skill and devious disrespect of a Don Juan persuades one of the mourners, Lady Anne, herself a recent widow, to marry him. Later he has her killed so that he is free to strengthen his position for the throne by marrying Elizabeth of York. His treachery, his deceptive use of women, his clutch of every evil device eventually bring him to the crown, which he then accepts with a repulsive display of pious hypocrisy. But after smothering little children in their beds, killing his wife and a host of others, and bringing a nation to civil war, Richard is crushed by the tragic consequences of his deeds and reduced to bargain for his life by shouting, "A horse! A horse! My kingdom for a horse!"

Modern literature, in contrast to this Elizabethan concern for willful defiance as the source of the tragic, has shifted to an exploration of the victim motif. In contrast to the ancient classic story, in which the hero was the tragic victim of the cosmic forces of fate, many writers today describe tragedy in terms of a psychological breakdown. The characters in the plays of Tennessee Williams are dangerously close to patients in a psychiatric ward. Evil is thrust upon them as a psychological sickness, which, no less than the classic demise, is fatefully incurable. Twisted and confused, the neurotic antiheros are condemned neither to death nor to hell but to live on in tortured anguish, victimized and possessed by strange, irrational, interior forces which are never resolved.

The novels of Franz Kafka illustrate this modern appreciation for the objective and irrational element in the evil that is thrust upon us. Kafka writes of the ironic absurdity of the human predicament. In his novel *The Castle*, Kafka describes with serious joy and pathetic humor the ridiculous situation of a land surveyor. The character, whom he gives the anonymous appellation K, at least thinks he is a land surveyor, although he is never quite sure what he has been called to do. This is his problem: he wants to work, he knows he must do something and he wants to do what is required of him, yet he can never establish contact with his employer, the lord of the castle. He tries every device to discover the will of the lord. Sometimes they are comic, sometimes they are tragic, but always his efforts are absurd, futile, and self-destroying. At one time he comes to a tavern where he learns the telephone number of the master. He is told he may try to get a connection, but that others have tried before, and no one has succeeded. With plodding courage he rings up the number and, miracle of miracles, the operator gives him a clear signal. With his heart in his throat and pulses pounding he waits to hear the voice of the lord, but all he can hear is the sound of little children, laughing.

Kafka is saying that the inexorable fate of man is that he is doomed to work in a society which never gives him satisfaction for his work. He hopes to get this in any way possible, from his boss, or his colleagues, or his girl Amalia, or his community, or even, and especially, from God. But the grim joke is that there is no satisfaction, because ultimately there is no God, only little children laughing at him. Kafka presents a protest against the inhuman depersonalization of the machine age and its political bureaucracy, but his message plunges more deeply into the essential tragedy of human existence. More than a psychoneurotic patient, more than a social pawn, man is the tragic victim of a terrible cosmic breach in which he is cut off from the source of his being so that he feels an inescapable guilt for his past, though he does not know what he has done, and a frightening horror for the future, because he is forced to believe against his will that there is no future. All this is because the circumstances of his life, within and without, tell him that where he should find the source of his being there is only nothing.

What we are confronted with in modern literature is a crisis of identity. Evil manifests itself in social sickness and psychological pain because men are lost from themselves and from their fellows and from God. Arthur Miller has written two plays in which he wrestles courageously with the problem of identity. He sees, as Søren Kierkegaard saw in *The Sickness unto Death,* that evil is the anguish of two kinds of despair, the despair of extraversion and the despair of introversion.

In *Death of a Salesman,* Willy Loman stalks inevitably to suicide because he desperately tries to be someone he is not. Not knowing who he is, not satisfied with anything within him, he becomes crazed with an obsession to be successful in acquiring things outside himself. He is the outgoing type who lives on a smile and a shoestring. His life is a hollow deceit. His boss has no time for him except as he is a productive salesman. His children are duped to live along with his lie. Even his wife contributes to his sham with the emptiness of her sentimental self-pity. At the end, his elder son comes to a late understanding of the problem. In the shock of despair he cries out to his father: "All I want is out there waiting for me the minute I say I know who I am. Why can't I say that, Willy?"[3] The father's loss of identity was reflected in the son, who shared in the tragedy as sin rips through from generation to generation. This is the sin of trying to be what we are not.

Miller's second play, *A View from the Bridge,* is not so individualistically existential. The tragedy is not simply in the person of the hero himself, who invites his own doom. Willy in *Death of a Salesman* becomes anxiously narrowed by covering himself with a false mask, but

[3] *Death of a Salesman* (New York: Viking, 1949), p. 132.

Eddie in *A View from the Bridge* is wholly open. His tragedy is not in deceiving himself and others. It is in trying to be himself alone without any others. A lawyer functions as the Greek chorus in the play, and he remarks at the end that one of the redeeming things about Eddie is the openness with which he gave himself up to the tragedy that crushed him. His guilt was his own, but there was also the dark nemesis of an inevitable situation that kept building up and from which there was no release because he could never settle for a halfway solution. Again identity is lost, but instead of the self's being lost to a perverted and prideful extraversion as in the earlier play, now identity is lost through a stubborn determination to turn inward to oneself (Luther's *cor incurvatus in se*) at the expense of all others. The truth of our human tragedy is that we cannot be what we are with or without others.

Only God has written the play in which the chief character is truly himself, and not what he or others want to make him. Jesus is presented in the Gospel story as the one man among all men who really knew who he was. No man took his life away from him; he laid it down of himself, and when he died he knew that he was the one who had come from God and who was also forsaken by God. He also knew the reason why he was forsaken, because he had taken upon himself our sinful flesh. But unlike that of every other tragic hero, his despair was victory because he died without relinquishing his identity, although throughout his life, and especially at the end, he was sorely tempted to do so. Yet he died committing his spirit to God the Father and not to the devil or to nothingness or to any other falsehood. In his victorious death he revealed that life is truly not work but gift. He came as one sent from the Father. He lived cheerfully, without anxiety for the morrow, as one who steadfastly affirmed his own being. He died in

the constant trust that God would receive him. This is
the strange and wonderful story in which the tragedy
is not denied or diverted but is affirmed and conquered
by a triumphant turn at the end.

The theme of evil as thrust upon man as a victim is
not a modern invention. Indeed the psychological collapse and the irrational forces pictured in contemporary
novels and plays are more graphically portrayed in the
literary history of the Satan figure. It may be that the
figure of Satan is the more profound narrative way of
communicating the reality of victimization in the tragedy of human existence. When Satan is understood within the context of the story, and when he is not reduced
with wooden literalness to a contradictory historical apparition, then he gains the integrity of a reality that is
larger than history. It is in this fashion that the devil was
conceived by Dante, Milton, Goethe, and in our day by
Charles Williams. Not that these authors all told the
same story or that their demonic characters are the same.
There are significant differences between the Satan of
Dante and the Mephistopheles of Goethe. Dante's devil
is the ruler of hell and the punisher of evildoers. This
strangely unbiblical view apparently captured the imagination of the Medieval Christian world and was not
challenged by the Protestant Puritanism of John Milton.
Nevertheless it is not a true story, in this respect, although it has many qualities of truth that bring it into
close harmony with the Christian story.

The truth in Dante's story is the picture of Satan as
the rebel who was cast out of heaven and who, having
usurped the kingdom of this world and having tempted
man, has become the painful source of all evil. The role
of torturer, visiting the punishment of God's wrath upon
wicked sinners, is a Medieval invention of a most curious
nature. The ancient world, neither biblical nor pagan,

the Oriental world, and now the modern world have found no truth in it.

Goethe, for example, departed radically from this Medieval notion when in *Faust* he pictures the devil as the goad to progress. The old myth of the bargain for man's soul is used. The terms are that if ever Faust should stop in his search for truth and be satisfied with what he has, his soul must go to the devil. And after he has seen the face of Helen and all the wonders of the ancient world, after he has learned the truths of science and the techniques of industry, after he has established himself as a great and benevolent tycoon of the modern world, he looks out on his valley where he has built homes for his workers, and seeing the smoke swirling from their chimneys he dreams of the happiness of the families inside, and is content. This he would like to keep, and forgetting his bargain he says, "*Verweile doch, du bist so schön!*"

Whence comes the tragedy in *Faust?* There is evil because man is cursed to seek forever and never to hold the truth, yet this is an ambiguous evil because the search produces progress and the holding produces death. The tragedy is that man will always grow weary and become content. Man is thus the victim of a demonic power that both drives him onward in an unrequited search and withers his soul when he stops.

A most profound, though brief, treatment of the Satan figure is presented by Charles Williams in his one-act play *House by the Stable*. Here Satan is bluntly called Hell. He is a guest in the house of Man. The guest is entertained by playing cards, using a precious jewel, man's soul, as the stake. Man shows a flippant disrespect for his precious jewel, but the devil shows a cunning determination to have it. Instead of the punisher of sinners or the ruler of hell or the goad to progress, this satanic figure is a liar and a cheat. He tempts man and tries to win over him by trickery. In this respect he is closer to the biblical story than any of the monumental and epic treatments that have come from former generations. As the ruler of this world he is received in the house of Man as an honored guest. But the devil's trickery is miraculously and ironically interrupted just as he is about to win the game when Man is startled to keen awareness by the sudden cry of a newborn child in the stable beside the house. The devil's fraud is exposed and Man's soul is saved.

Evil in this story is due to the cooperation of man with another who is neither himself nor God. We return here to the complex story in which tragedy is highly ambiguous and complicated by the combination of the rebel and the victim motifs. Man is both flippant and defiant, the devil is cunning and treacherous. Man's tragedy is that he is anguished and possessed.

Perhaps the best presentation of the meaning of evil can be found among the novels of Dostoevsky, and particularly in the novel which he called *The Possessed*. This is a story told from the human side alone, without the nonhistorical or nonhuman figures. But with subtle artistry Dostoevsky describes men and women who freely exercise their wills while at the same time being possessed by the rankest demonism.

*The Possessed* is the story of Stavrogin, a dashing young noble who is fabulously rich and the darling of elite society in late nineteenth-century Russia. He is loved and respected by everyone, but as the story unfolds we learn that he hardly justifies his reputation. He has raped a fourteen-year-old girl. He has secretly married a half-witted crippled peasant out of sheer perversity on a dare. He has seduced a beautiful society girl and then repudiated her, driving her half-crazed to her death by a murderous mob. He has begotten a child by another man's wife. And all the while he has been the idol of a political revolutionary whose devilish schemes have brought ruin on the entire community. Stavrogin finally hangs himself, but not until he has indirectly brought about six murders, two suicides, and three natural deaths that are produced by circumstances which may be laid at his feet.

This is a story of rebellion. There is tension between the generations in which the son, Peter Verkhovensky, rebels violently against the petty bourgeois idealism of his father. There is tension between the classes, with the intellectuals and the workers rising against the nobles and the landowners. There is defiance against traditional conventions and established morality, with the institutions of church and state and marriage and property viciously attacked by new forces of nihilism.

This is also the story of the possessed. Good people with noble intentions and high ideals who will sacrifice themselves with selfless tenderness become victims of circumstance in which they find themselves doing criminal deeds which would make the devil blush.

Such is the nature of evil. Man is both anguished and possessed, a defiant rebel who is personally guilty for his crimes and at the same time a confused victim who is caught in the cunning trap of the devil's tempting treachery.

# II

## Looking for Love

Of all the themes that literature and religion hold in common, the theme of love should certainly provide helpful insight for the thesis that story is the key to reality. This is especially true of Christianity, which is often called the religion of love. It should be a most fruitful field of investigation today, when most novels and plays are love stories.

The theme of love, however, presents a serious problem, because love has so many faces. The word "love" is used in different contexts to mean a variety of things, some of which are almost direct opposites to each other. Love can mean the desire or aspiration to lift oneself to the heights of ideal perfection, or it can mean the lowering of oneself in sacrificial devotion to serve where there is need. Love can mean emotional abandon or it can mean disciplined devotion. It can mean personal sacrifice or it can mean sacrifice of persons. It can mean harmless playful entertainment and it can mean hurtful exploitative lust. Love is truly "a many-splendored thing."

Ancient pagan love was founded in the Aphrodite myth. At first in the chthonic cults love was conceived in terms of the male deity Eros, but later love was understood to be served from Olympus by a goddess. When Cronus wounded Father Sky in the great battle between the Olympians and the Titans, drops of blood fell upon the sea. From the foam that rose around the blood, a lovely girl was formed. Her name was Aphrodite, which means rising from the foam. Glowing with tender beauty, she was pictured by the Romans as Venus and by the Orientals as Lakshmi or Kuan Yin. Lakshmi characteristically floated on a lotus blossom. The stories spun around these deities varied, of course, in different cultures from the theme of love as natural attraction to merciful compassion. The Chinese Kuan Yin and Japanese Kwannon stories developed originally from Indian tales of a male god, but in Buddhism, after the Christian era, the Mahayana sect incorporated an emotional element which paralleled both the Madonna devotion of Medieval Christianity and the fundamental Christian concept of compassion which comes from above.

In Greece the love theme developed along two lines, one more intellectual and the other more narrative, just as did their understanding of evil. In Plato's *Symposium* love is presented as a feast of many foods, but the richest and most tasty is described by Socrates as intellectualized desire (eros) for the completion of one's being. As he is, man is incomplete, imperfect, fretfully wandering and searching for the fulness his life lacks. This accounts for the attraction of the sexes, for according to an old myth man was originally a monosexual creature with four arms and four legs, but somehow he was split in two and hence we have males and females as only half creatures each seeking fulfillment in the other half. But Plato thought the attraction of the sexes to be very low on the ladder of love. Indeed in his estimation the love of man for woman is not higher than the love of man for man. True love is not biological at all, nor is it romantic. These levels of love easily fall into profane sensuality. Love, seen as the aspiration for fulness of being, is described as the child of Want and Plenty. Man is in want, lacking perfection. True being is full and complete and perfect. Love is the desire in man to reach for fulness and perfection. Love is striving for self-realization. In a broad sense love is then the profound appreciation for real beauty in both male and female, and ultimately, as this ideal is pushed to the extreme, in God. Sacred love then became the basis for conduct, and a culture was built upon it. Through the influence of Origen and Augustine, this notion was brought into the Christian scheme of things and played a prominent role throughout Western civilization.

Another understanding of love was recorded in the great narrative epics of ancient Greece. This is the notion of faithfulness (*philia*), which in the breach prompted the tragedy of the Trojan war and in the honoring, the perseverance of Odysseus. *The Iliad* and *The Odyssey* are not usually seen as love stories. They are tales of the heroism of warriors, like the Anglo-Saxon epic of Beowulf and the Teutonic tales of Siegfried. But Helen was the face that launched the thousand ships, and Penelope was the faithful wife who waited for twenty years for the return of her husband. While Penelope was hounded by her suitors, Odysseus was pursued by the wrath of Poseidon, driven from one trial to another until finally after shipwreck and harrowing escape from the one-eyed monster Polyphemus, after release from both the divine temptress Circe and the humanly tender Nausicaa, this harrowed adventurer crosses the wine dark sea to his kingdom of Ithaca and the loving arms of Penelope. Love as faithfulness is a quality of the good, but more deeply understood it is the dramatic action and passion in which a man and a woman will cleave to each other despite all odds until they die.

Here is the bridge between pagan and Hebrew culture. For the ancient Hebrews love is the story of Ruth, who left her homeland for her husband. The notion of love as fulfillment was also important for the Hebrews. It is not good that man should be alone. When a man marries, he must leave his father and mother and cleave to his wife, and the two become one flesh. But faithfulness and the breach of it dominate the stories of Abraham, David, and Esther. Moreover, the fulfillment in the biblical injunction is not the philosophical completion of one's being, but the satisfying of a relationship which actually involves emptying oneself.

The grand Christian notion of love as sacrifice (*agape*) is thus presaged in the story of Hosea and Gomer. Hosea cleaves to his wife even though she is a faithless prostitute. His tenderness is mocked as he sacrifices himself for her. This sacrificial love of service, mercy, and compassion has become in the Christian story the basis not only for marriage, but for all community life and for the deepest understanding of the relation between God and man in the church. Christians enter into marriage as a holy estate, a sacramental communion in which they are devoted to each other as Christ loved the church and gave himself for it. Christians in community are exhorted to love each other as Christ loved them. Christians are even charged to love their enemies as God loved sinners who in enmity crucified his Son. Christian love is not man's aspiration toward perfection, though it may be a striving in one sense. It is an inspiration toward service, in which we live not for ourselves but for others. If it is a striving, it is a joyful, careless, celebrative action born of gratitude. There is dramatic irony in that in the practice of Christian love one receives only in giving. We are filled with love when we empty ourselves.

Two things happened in the story of Christianity which prevented a full flowering of this seed of sacrificial love: the early Christian preoccupation with the imminent coming of the Final Judgment, and the marriage of Platonic idealism with Pauline theology. The concern for the End prompted Paul to say that all else must be secondary — even marriage must be sacrificed to a complete attention to Christ's return. Only to avoid lustful temptations was marriage to be tolerated. This, coupled with the Platonic rationalization that spiritual love is superior to carnal sensuality, gave celibacy precedence over marriage in the Medieval scheme of values. Although this was clearly a perversion of the Christian understanding of love, even in the more profound insights of Paul himself, the severe repression of sexuality which resulted has so strongly insinuated itself into Christian culture, both Catholic and Protestant, that several revolutions have not been able to shake it. The first and most violent revolt came with the advent of chivalric romanticism. This was followed by the smaller waves of the Renaissance, and then the Restoration, and now the current breaker which, as in the past, may only produce a reactionary undertow that will carry us out to sea again.

Through all the febrile attempts to justify and even sanctify marriage, there has persisted the notion that celibacy is a superior course of action. This is supposedly because the love of God should have no rival. In reaching to be filled with God, the faithful lover renounces devotion to all else. But this exclusiveness derives from the simplistic monism and mysticism of Plato, whose God draws us all upward and inward to himself. The Christian story tells of one who comes to us and gives himself for us so that when we give ourselves to him we give ourselves to others. Christian love is never exclusive nor ideally celibate. One might wonder why it should be monogamous, but the answer to this question is quickly settled by pragmatic considerations.

This perverted Christian morality really denied sexual love since it was tolerated only within the marriage bond, and then only as a means to procreate children. In the eleventh century the romantic cult of chivalric love arose in reaction. This ideal fought the church and provided a secular base for culture until a new foundation was found in the classical humanism of the Renaissance. Thus in the fifteenth century Malory, fearing that the chivalric code would die, wrote nostalgically about it in *Le Morte Darthur,* and in the beginning of the seventeenth century Cervantes, fearing the code of the knight errant would never die, wrote satirically about it in *Don Quixote* so as to give it the *coup de grace.*

Before Christianity the epic sagas of the north told of the fierce Anglo-Saxon ideals of courage, self-honor, and loyalty to one's leader. "Death is better for every man than a life of shame," says Wiglaf to his cowardly companions in *Beowulf.* All events were played out against the fundamental belief in a highly imaginative nature folklore plus the fatalism of the inexorable *Wyrd.*

With the coming of Christianity, at least two major changes came to the foundation belief of Western Europe, although it cannot be denied that much of the folklore and the fatalism was never completely overthrown. But the Christian faith in the resurrection and the faith that God loves the sinner radically changed the heroic warrior of the pagan world. Of the joyful hope in the resurrection the pagan world knew nothing. Only the heroes who died in battle could enter Valhalla, and this was a dark abode of shadow shapes like the Hades of the Greeks. The new Christian faith, however, sang a song of triumph, and this produced a new literature in the miracle plays. About that we shall speak later, when we deal with the theme of hope. The second change came from the new faith that God loves sinners. The old heroism of warriors could hardly survive in such a climate, and an interesting sublimation and rationalization of the combat instinct occurred. Now the knight in shining armor did not fight for his homeland; he went forth in

fealty to his lady and his liege-lord to fight for the love
of God. He became an errant knight and a crusader.

The radical shift from the warrior folk-hero to the
errant knight can be pictured if you will imagine how
ridiculous Beowulf would have looked fawning obse-
quiously over his lady's hand and taking her scented
handkerchief with him as he stalks the monster Grendel.
The old pagan world regarded women as ornaments or
chattels or marriageable commodities. Now the Christian faith and the cult of the Virgin raised women to the
place of the feudal lord. Feudal courtly love reversed
the ancient pattern so that instead of man's dominating
and using woman, he served her with abject humility
as if he were her vassal. In fiction, if not in daily life,
the knight worshipped woman because Mary was a woman. He bound himself to his fair damsel by oaths of
homage and fealty and would rather die than be faithless.

At least so it was at first. But the new love brought by
Christianity, if you will remember, was bound in a strait-
jacket. Because the moral apparatus of the church in
practice offered no positive sexual outlet, feudal courtly
love took a turn in the songs and visions of the troubadours, which not only secularized love but actually
glorified adultery. The romantic love of the troubadours
could never be realized by two married persons because
this love must be given freely, while in marriage love is
given as a matter of duty and constraint. Therefore they
sang with triumphant gusto when a knight would woo
another man's lady.

The Arthurian romances exhibit the various historical
forces congealing: the old Anglo-Saxon heritage, the
Celtic folk-heroes, the new French minstrelsy after the
Norman conquest, the new chivalric code, the virtues
of honor and fealty, and the daring adultery. The Celtic
Gawain is the picture of the sun god whose strength

waxes till noon and then wanes. The Celtic Tristram provides the pinnacle of chivalrous love in his adulterous devotion to Isoud. But Lancelot towers over all because he is of French origin and French minstrelsy originated the chivalric revolt.

The reaction of the church to the tales of adulterous love in such heroes and heroines as Lancelot and Guinevere and Tristram and Isoud is interesting. Instead of censoring the loose tales of the worldly troubadours, the church took their heroes and refashioned the stories into moral romances having a didactic aim. Perhaps the most felicitous example of this is *Sir Gawain and the Green Knight*. Gawain was a Welsh hero who proved himself in a double test for courage and chastity, thus combining the two themes of Medieval culture, namely warrior heroism and chivalric love, but regenerating both into the feudal ideals of personal honor and Christian chastity. Another example is the sequel to the Lancelot saga in the Sir Galahad romance, in which the quest is not for an illicit liaison but for divine love symbolized by the Holy Grail. Galahad is not a legendary figure but a spiritual ideal personified. Love is not merely purified from adulterous romance to chaste fidelity, it is sublimated and desexed into a religious virtue. Many of these moral romances were clumsy and the didacticism was obtrusive and artificial, but others were artfully done and the power and success of the church's strategy may be measured by the fact that this threefold combination of moral didacticism with the themes of romantic love and the warrior hero is still the basis for the modern Western. In the melodrama of cinema and television, the daring desperado is the modern counterpart of the ancient monster, the dragon slain by the courageous knight. The modern knight is often a lawman, to indicate further the symbolism of the fight for justice. The women are always fair and pure, while evil resides in men or gangs of men. And the moralism is drawn so as to leave no room for ambiguity. We still consider this the criterion of acceptability. No literature is censored if it exhibits an edifying moral, even if it has no aesthetic quality or even if it speaks to no universal human need.

The intrusion of love was longer in coming as a theme for the theater than in the songs of the minstrels. This was largely because women were not yet accepted as actors on the stage even in the Tudor period. Shakespeare's *As You Like It* is typical of the Renaissance approach to love. It is playful entertainment. Since there were no actresses on the stage and all the female parts had to be played by boys or men with falsetto voices, all seriousness in the love drama was lost. The French bedroom farce and the current boy-gets-girl comedies also exhibit the light side of love. But the persistent popularity of this nondidactic treatment of love as a basic human emotion indicates that in spite of its sentimentality there is something in the triumph of love that is worthy of our respect.

With the appearance of Don Juan in Tirso de Molina's play *The Trickster of Seville and the Guest of Stone,* in 1630, we have the beginning of a new myth with a most fascinating literary history. Don Juan is truly a myth even though it is late in origin compared to the myths of Prometheus, Odysseus, Faust, or Tristram. As we have seen in the discussion on evil, the Don Juan theme is about the tragedy of defiance. It is not really a love story, but yet it owes its existence and meaning to a certain attitude toward love. Don Juan is not the cynical amorist of Boccaccio, nor is he the passionate humanist of Petrarch. He comes out of the background of the chivalric love of the troubadours in his defiant breach of chastity and fidelity. He shares the troubadours' low opinion of marriage, but he is also contemptuous of the honest passion of romance. He is a corruption of Tristram. Molina's Don Juan is a figure of oleaginous flattery and headspinning lyricism. He seduces both ladies and wenches without any real affection for any of his conquests. Unlike Tristram, whose love is a swooning desire for desire that tragically knows it cannot be fulfilled, Don Juan rejects the satisfaction of both marriage and romance for the crude satisfaction of physical accomplishment. His love is sneering and contemptuous. Again, as we have seen, his greatest pleasure is to disadvantage and dishonor women, all of which is ultimately a gesture of defiance against God. Thus after Don Juan has killed Dona Ana's father, the father returns in the stony guise of a famous statue and drags Don Juan down to hell for a retribution which Don Juan prefers to divine obeisance.

Molina's Don Juan is presented in a drama which is essentially a morality play in defense of God and the virtue of Christian love. Don Juan is a villainous rogue who got his just deserts for his exploitative lust. In the eighteenth century a shift in attitude developed. Already the earlier treatments of Molière and the libretto of Mozart's *Don Giovanni* by Lorenzo da Ponte show sympathy for Don Juan in accord with the new rationalism and its rebellion against the supernatural. Instead of his being the arch villain, he is the hero. Whereas the original Don Juan believed in God but defied him, the new Don Juan had a rationalist contempt for God, marriage, and women. Byron's Don Juan laughs not at God and death, but more superficially and sentimentally he mocks respectability.

In the nineteenth century we have still another twist. Instead of Don Juan doing the rebelling, we have Dona Juana. The great rebels against society are women. Emma Bovary is the patron saint of the frail sisterhood of erring wives. Becky Sharp and Anna Karenina are furies of emotional independence, avenging male inade-

quacy. Instead of being the innocent victims of Don
Juan's seduction, the new heroines seduce more than
they are seduced. There is a return to the original Christian story of Eve as the archtemptress, a theme long neglected in both the Medieval ideal of the Virgin and the
Protestant bourgeois virtue of virginity. The middle
class had tended to view woman as pure and man as the
source of evil, but now the concern is to break all conventions for men and women. Sentimental rebellious
romance now gave way to feminist domination. Miss
Anne Whitefield in Shaw's *Man and Superman* is the
devious trickster, reversing roles with Jack Tanner, who
is no longer the pursuer but the pathetic pursued. Miss
Anne hunts him down with every wile, even the ultimate deception of feminine weakness. Love is the life
force in petticoats, and rebellion is the pusillanimous
moralizing of the irreverent liberal.

Since Shaw literature has been preoccupied with sex
or violence. Since the old God is dead and no new God
has risen to take his place, literature can neither defy the
old God nor extol a new one. Consequently much of
modern literature dwells with rhapsodic lyricism upon
sexual intercourse as the only fulfillment of love. D. H.
Lawrence's *Lady Chatterley's Lover* illustrates this fre-
netic concern for sexual fulfillment as the only means of
redeeming an otherwise empty life. Since Lady Chatterley cannot be physically satisfied by her husband, she
raises the moral question of why she should not find satisfaction outside her marriage. This is a legitimate question for ethical debate, and we will consider it later in
our discussion of the quest for holiness, but it is not the
reason for the sale of the book. The prurient interest in
the detailed description of the sex act is the reason for
its success.

Literature today treats love itself, not just women or
God or morality, with utter contempt. It does this either

by the sheer exploitation of love, from cheap novels like
*The Carpetbaggers* to the sophisticated clinical dissec-
tion of love by James Gould Cozzens in *By Love Possessed*, or by contemptuously ignoring love altogether,
as in the great works of Melville and Conrad.

We have run a great gamut in the literary history of
the theme of love. We have seen some of the many facets
of love to be the metaphysical desire for completion of
one's being, faithfulness, sacrificial compassion, romantic chivalry, moral chastity, playful entertainment, passionate human sentiment, exploitative defiant lust, and
the physical satisfaction of biological desire. Today most
novels and plays are love stories in which respect for
love itself is lost because the original defiance has slipped
into the cynical despair of nihilism. Characters jump
from partner to partner with increasing anguish because
in their purposeless confusion they persist in seeking
psychological satisfaction in a physical act. But love
will not die. No matter how badly love is treated, whether in savage contempt or in bitter neglect, there is a
reality in love that wins its way into the stories men tell.
Once more we find that story provides a clear and compelling insight into the nature of reality.

It is shocking to observe that love in its literary history has a remarkable parallel to the force of evil. Love
ironically becomes a source of the tragic in human existence. The pursuit of love produces pain. Love, which
is called the action of God for our salvation, becomes
the power that breaks communication and brings ultimate tragedy. Yet, through the tragedy the triumph of
love rings true. Men will pursue it in spite of its pain.

This is true for both sick love and genuine love. That
sick love brings pain is obvious. The moralism of this
theme has been exhibited in novels and on stage and
screen *ad nauseam*. Freudian analysis of the sickness of
repressed love has probably been more fruitful in its

literary use than as scientific therapy. The warped love
portrayed by Tennessee Williams in plays like *A Street-
car Named Desire, Summer and Smoke,* and *Cat on a
Hot Tin Roof* is neatly packaged pain from the super-
market of Freudian mythology. Mai Zetterling's screenplay *Night Games* displays with arresting candor how a
twisted, self-indulgent mother-love can prevent a boy
from growing to be a man. So long as the Freudian moral
is served, no limits can be placed upon the documen-
tary exposé of the perversion. Pornography cannot be
be charged if all comes out right in the end, and "coming
out right" in this case means a righteous resolution in
accordance with a set of Freudian moral values. If the
childhood trauma can be isolated and then exposed,
the painful repression can be removed and the natural
force of love can have free expression. While the Freudian theme may be doubted as a scientific theory since
it lacks experimental substantiation, it cannot be denied
that it is a myth, since it supplies genuine food for
stories, howbeit a shallow myth which appears to be
rather ephemeral.

A totally different treatment of perverted love, however, is beginning to come from the so-called underground films. The most significant of these is Andy Warhol's *The Chelsea Girls.* Here love is presented without
obeisance to either the Victorian code or the Freudian.
Original techniques in filming are used to make the
message less obvious and therefore more subtle and sug-
gestive. Deliberate blurring of the sound track makes
the dialogue ambiguous. The screen is divided and two
sequences are shown simultaneously, with both dialogue
and characters occasionally passing from one side to the
other. Some of the closeups are designed to titillate the
viewer as he might be if he were on an excursion with
psychedelic drugs, and the whole movie is an arty doc-
umentary of different kinds of social deviation under

the influence of narcotics. The message is that love is
free, that to be free is to love, and to be free means to be
bound by no code except honesty to one's own emotions.
In this view there can be no rejection of any kind of
love, nor of any expression of love, so long as it is the
honest expression of the love partners' desires. Using the
narcotic needle seems to be necessary to break down
outdated barriers of conscience, but more profoundly, in
this new quest for love the desire is to indulge one's own
emotions to such an extreme that it becomes necessary
to obliterate the outside world, even to the extent of ob-
literating one's own love partner. Dope makes it possible to experience in the realm of fantasy a fuller physical
satisfaction without exploiting another. In Warhol's film
there is no statement of retributive justice such as we
find in Victorian and Freudian ethics. There is simply
the morality of protest, the protest of the slave breaking
his shackles with his fevered mind obsessed by the single sick thought: I want to be free to do whatever I want.

The sickness of love brings pain, but more profoundly
and more poignantly the health of genuine love is tragic. Perhaps the best example of this in recent literature
is the story of *Dr. Zhivago*. Boris Pasternak's novel is a
love story above all. The thousands of Russians who
filed by in mourning at Pasternak's grave, just as he described in his story the silent respect for the poet Yuri
Zhivago, together with the universal acclaim on both
sides of the iron curtain, give proof that human love
transcends partisan politics. This is a story of war between classes, of revolution and counterrevolution. This
is a story of great upheaval in which social values struggle for precedence over individual rights. This is a story
of types, different kinds of people who make up a world.
But primarily it is a love story showing the many faces
of love.

The story of *Dr. Zhivago* tells how a bloody, brutish

revolution transformed Russia from an idyllic feudal farm into a progressive, industrial city. Fearful attempts to preserve a crumbling social structure produced in the Czarist masters a savage brutality which trampled on the little people demanding to be treated as persons instead of property. Yet when the revolution came and these same little people became the masters, their ruthless revenge and programmed organizing of the new society was even more savage. But when the dust of the battle had settled, there emerged a city in which great machines were now doing the work of puny man, and everybody's position has been shuffled. Although it is not sure whether each man's new place is really better, it is certain that only a few, and they are very old, want to go back to the old society.

Three types of men are described in *Dr. Zhivago.* Komarovsky is the unprincipled opportunist, evil to the core. Exploitative lust is his consuming drive. He is a bourgeois businessman who has made a fortune exploiting bourgeois society, but he has no scruples against sliding into the rising Communist scheme of things and exploiting the new society for money and position. He is the same with love. His lust for Lara makes her his mistress when she is only seventeen, though it is the same lust that brings him to her rescue when she is threatened by her dead husband's enemies. And her husband, Strelnikov, is the opposite type to Komarovsky. He is the principled absolutist, pure and incorruptible. He has a gyroscope built inside him which drives him forward in a single path with such fury that he will run down anybody in the way of his dream. So devoted is he to his ideal that he leaves havoc in his wake as he pursues it. Yuri Zhivago is the third type, a confused, vacillating soul like most of us, who is caught between these extremes of rampant evil and ruthless purity. Yuri has no great ideal, no consuming passion. He simply wants to be himself, to be left alone to pursue his little loves and to find satisfaction in his work. He is the man Paul describes in the seventh chapter of Romans: the good he would do he does not, and the evil he would not he does. The social upheaval swirls around him and he vaguely sees its implications, but his great concerns are more immediate, and perhaps therefore more abiding. He must be warm so that his hands can write the poetry in his soul.

But the story is really about love. We have noticed that Komarovsky's love for Lara is an abusive lust, but that this same selfish love prompts him to offer refuge to Lara and escape for Yuri. Neither could accept without being compromised, but Lara had to go with him for the sake of Yuri's child, and Yuri had to refuse because he was too weak to fight any more.

Yuri's love for Lara is desire, not exploitative, not even sought, but an emotional compulsion that is thrust upon both as an irrepressible mystery. Yuri's love for Tonya, his wife, is no less honest, no less tender, though perhaps less physical and more intellectual. They are companions. She can appreciate and understand his poetry, Lara cannot; yet it is Lara who inspires the verse. The love for the two women is genuine but different. That a man can love two women is not denied, it is affirmed without reservation; but so is the pain this causes in the hearts of all three.

There is sacrifice in this love too. Certainly the love is mixed in all the characters. Lara will sacrifice anything for Zhivago, even her own integrity when she is so caught by circumstances that she can no longer stay with Zhivago but must go with Komarovsky to save Yuri's child. Tonya's love is patient and forgiving since she knows she must sacrifice for the poet in Yuri.

Love is what carries the characters to their highest joys, their abiding concerns, and also their deepest sor-

rows. They will love, and go on loving, even if it means
cruel pain to themselves and others; but through all the
tragedy there is a triumph of love that makes the tragedy worthwhile. It is as if the stories of the little loves of
little people are enclosed in a greater story of a greater
love that will win in the end despite all the grim opposi-
tion it receives on the way. The device of the story within
a story is indeed what we find in Robert Bolt's screenplay
of *Dr. Zhivago,* for this is the story of the various
loves of many people enclosed in another story, the love
of Yevgrav for his brother Yuri Zhivago, and his search
for Yuri's and Lara's daughter. The story within a story,
the world within a world, is a literary structure found in
many cultures in many ages — in the Arabian *Shehere-
zade,* in Boccaccio's *Decameron,* in Shakespeare's *Hamlet,* in Brecht's *Caucasian Chalk Circle,* in Albee's *Tiny
Alice,* and in Wasserman's *Man of La Mancha,* to name
a few. It would seem that we have here the clue to a
greater love than all the loves of history, than all the
loves in nature, than all the love in the myriads of stories that are told. There is a story of love which embraces
them all and in which every story finds its place, but
this greater love purges the loves of men and nature,
cleansing and renewing them until they really come
alive in the triumph of love which transcends all evil
and defeat and death. There is a love which moves us
and lifts us in every way, physically, mentally, emotion-
ally, spiritually, a love which gives us a part in a play,
a love which produces a story that has its pain but
gains for us meaning and new life.

# III

## The Quest for Holiness

There is a quest for holiness in the scheme of things, a universal striving to be right. There has long been a debate over whether the right and the good are eternal verities that obtain in all times and all places for all people, or whether what is right and good varies with cultures according to relative and positivistic codes. And today it is being questioned whether morality does not vary not only with cultures but with the particular circumstances we find ourselves in. But never has it been questioned that some actions are good and others bad, some actions are right and others wrong; and more profoundly that some actions are less evil than others. As Thomas Jefferson observed: "It is the melancholy law of human societies to be compelled sometimes to choose a great evil in order to ward off a greater evil."

The words "right," "just," "good," "holy" have a variety of uses. "Right" is etymologically Anglo-Saxon. It means in its origin to be straight, as opposed to being crooked. To be morally upright means to stand straight and not be bent or fallen. In this sense it is synonymous with "true," as an arrow is straight and true. There is a functional semantics here. What is right is straight and true in the purpose for which it is intended. Right is done when a straight arrow is sent true to its mark. Morality

is doing the truth, keeping one's troth, pursuing straight
to the mark. Immorality is failing, falling, and missing
the mark (*hamartia*, sin in the biblical sense).

"Just," on the other hand, is Latin in origin. It means
to be correct in a legal sense. A just man is one who conforms to the law, and in a broader sense the law itself
is just when it conforms to a standard or first principle of
justice. In ancient Roman society this principle of justice was *suum cuique*, to each his own. Every man was
to be given justice according to his deserts. Distribution
of wealth, social position, political favors, and all the
goods of life were ideally determined on this basis. If
a man were born a slave and deserved no better, his
fetters were considered just; but this did not preclude
his rising to become an emperor if his talents merited it.

Ultimately this principle of justice rested on the earlier
Greek definition of the good. Goodness was defined by
Socrates as a quality which inheres in objects themselves
regardless of how we esteem them. There is a hierarchy
of beings, with a broad base of lesser goods rising up in
pyramid fashion to the absolute good or *summum bonum*
at the peak. The quest for goodness is the intellectual
task of discerning the relative places of the various
goods, and gaining ultimate knowledge of the highest
good. In Greek usage, with all its metaphysical underpinnings, the good was understood in personal terms as
a quality of virtue. The good is the description of the
ideal man.

The Hebrew concept of goodness, before the legalism
of the Pharisees set in, was both functional and personal.
Unlike the Greek absolutism and like the Anglo-Saxon
functionalism, goodness was conceived by the Hebrews
in terms of actions and relationships. Things aren't good
in themselves. Things are good because God made them.
They are right when they have a relationship to him according to their place in his plan for the world. Right-

eousness is a relation between men and God and therefore also between men and each other and between men
and everything else in God's world. Righteousness is
doing God's will in relation to everyone and everything
we encounter.

In all cultures, however, behind and beneath the
quest for the right, the just, and the good is the sense of
the holy. Two strains of meaning coinhere in our usage
of the word "holy" — health and wholeness. To be holy
means to have health (*salus*, salvation) in the sense of
a well-being that satisfies the needful relationship with
God. It also means to be whole in the sense of not being
shredded or partial. To be whole is therefore to be different from all in this world that is fragmented, ephemeral,
and illusory. The holy is not of this world. It is different.
It is sacred as opposed to the profane, separated from
the fetid corruption outside the temple. It is religious as
opposed to the secular, dedicated to a course which does
not follow the world's sickness unto death.

This distinction between the sacred and the secular
is a real one, but it has been misunderstood and twisted
into a separation which current art forms are roundly
repudiating. Instead of being seen as different from
this world and its path from sin to death, the holy
was for centuries misconceived as being something out
of this world. Holiness was defined as an eternal verity
in a Platonic ideal heaven. Only some objects could be
holy, therefore, and they had to be removed as relics
to some sequestered place as far as possible from the din
of the world. Only some people could be holy, and they
too had to retire to monasteries or affect a religious
habit, both of dress and mien.

All this is being challenged today. Artists like Bon-
nard paint an ordinary breakfast table whereas in former centuries Leonardo painted the Last Supper. Any
object, any scene, any person is considered worthy of

celebration in artistic expression. We are returning to the original understanding of the holy according to which all things are good. But in this transitional period confusion arises because it is not clear why they are good.

One of the signs of our times is the new literature, which challenges the old value system without providing a positive substitute for what it rejects. *The Catcher in the Rye*, by J. D. Salinger, protests the phoniness of the adult world into which young Holden Caulfield is thrown, a world with a fixed morality that is outworn, artificial, meaningless. Holden breaks loose from his prep school in Pennsylvania, and from the fake world of adults, and goes underground in New York for three days. There he tries to be free, but lacking any new sense of responsibility, his rebellion becomes a sordid collapse. But the rebellion is honest, and he can never return to the hypocrisy of the past.

During one of his lonely reveries, he recalls the chapel services at school. Once an undertaker came and told the boys about prayer, what a good and holy thing is prayer. In Holden's words: "He told us we should always pray to God — talk to him and all — wherever we were. He told us we ought to think of Jesus as our buddy and all. He said *he* talked to Jesus all the time. Even when he was driving his car. That killed me. I can just see the big phony bastard shifting into first gear and asking Jesus to send him a few more stiffs."[1]

Since Holden Caulfield cannot accept the inanity of adult hypocrisy and since he cannot cope with his own irresponsibility, he recedes to the world of childhood innocence from which he came. He returns to his little sister Phoebe. He takes her to the park and gives her a ride on the carousel. While he is watching her it rains,

[1] *The Catcher in the Rye* (Boston: Little, Brown, 1951), p. 23.

a torrential rain which soaks him to the skin, but he does not care because it makes him so happy to see his sister riding around and around, looking so *damn* nice "in her blue coat and all."

There is a tugging, tearing pathos in this young boy's quest for holiness. He emerges from sleepy innocence to awakened wickedness like Prospero in W. H. Auden's *The Sea and the Mirror,* who says:

> When I awoke into my life, a sobbing dwarf
> Whom giants served only as they pleased, I was not
>   what I seemed;
>   Beyond their busy backs I made a magic
> To ride away from a father's imperfect justice,
> Take vengeance on the Romans for their grammar,
> Usurp the popular earth and blot out forever
>   The gross insult of being a mere one among
>     many.[2]

It seems that much of the literature of protest is just such an adolescent lament, the awakening of perceptive people to the world as it is. To their dismay, they find they are not what they thought they were, nor is the world. The revolution of our time is a transition to greater maturity, but in every revolution there is blood and breakage and excruciating pain.

The longing is for health and wholeness. This is how the pagan Greeks conceived holiness, as is evidenced by the ancient spa at Epidaurus. Surrounding a central temple dedicated to Esclapius, the god of healing, were a clinic for therapy, a dormitory for rest, a stadium for exercise, and a theater for the edification of the mind. Health was conceived as the cultivation of wholeness in the human person. Religion, art, physical culture, and medicine were aspects of a common discipline. This in-

[2] *The Sea and the Mirror* (London: Faber and Faber, 1945), p. 10.

tegration was gradually broken apart when Christians misunderstood their own heritage and made holiness an exclusively otherworldly concern. The Christian emperor Theodosius, for example, proscribed the Olympic games because they were associated with pagan religious festivals. In modern times the practice of medicine has become a secular profession instead of an eleemosynary service of the church. But the Christian view of holiness originally shared with the classic Greeks the notion of health and wholeness, and for this reason the current breakdown in morality should be welcomed as a necessary correction of an unfortunate historical deviation. The protest of Holden Caulfield is essentially a Christian protest, although he does not know it, because the Christian social system has become so artificial. Yet the basic story of reality says there is holiness, and it is health and wholeness, a straight and true action that is different from all else in the world. We have seen in modern times the development of both a literature of protest and a literature of revolt. Moral protest cries out against the duplicity and injustice in the conditions of contemporary society. Such protest may be levied against economic, social, political, or psychological conditions. Revolt, on the other hand, challenges not only the conditions but the principles which are considered ultimately responsible for the conditions.

The moral protest began with Swift and Voltaire. *Gulliver's Travels* exposes the foibles and fashions, customs and conventions of its age with merciless ridicule. Pompous self-delusion, artificiality, and blatant hypocrisy are the targets of Swift's attack. In *Candide* Voltaire goes deeper, because he challenges in his merry way the metaphysical underpinnings of a culture that had deceived itself into thinking this was the best of all possible worlds. Because of the philosophical complacency of the period, social and moral inequities were accepted with a lighthearted cruelty. Voltaire cut through all this bigotry by using his satirical pen as a sharp stiletto. Like Socrates, Voltaire wanted to come down out of the metaphysical heavens because, he insisted, the proper study of man is man.

With an awakened concern for humanitarian and social values, the moral protest was honed to razor sharpness for its attack upon the injustices of the rising industrial economy. From Dickens' *Oliver Twist* to Steinbeck's *The Grapes of Wrath* we hear the ancient prophetic protest of Amos, the shepherd of Tekoa, crying from the steps of the temple against the callousness, the blind greed, and the arrogant brutality of the masters in a society that has forgotten moral responsibility. The recent success of the musical play *Oliver* is testimony that this economic protest is still lively.

Social protest from *Uncle Tom's Cabin* to *Tobacco Road* has exposed the arrogant *hybris* of racism. Perhaps the most bitter blast has come from the French playwright Jean Genet in *The Blacks*: *A Clown Show*. In a preface the author says:

> This play, written . . . by a white man, is intended for a white audience, but if, which is unlikely, it is ever performed before a black audience, then a white person, male or female, should be invited every evening. The organizer of the show should welcome him formally, dress him in ceremonial costume and lead him to his seat, preferably in the front row of the orchestra. The actors will play for him. A spotlight should be focused upon this symbolic white throughout the performance.
>
> But what if no white person accepted? Then let white masks be distributed to the black spectators as they enter the theatre. And if the blacks refuse the masks, then let a dummy be used.

In a play within a play, a band of black players enacts before a jury of white-masked Negroes the ritualistic murder of a white person, a murder for which the Negroes have been accused. Characteristically for Genet, the jury is composed of a missionary bishop, an island governor-general, a judge, an arrogant queen, and her puny, mincing valet. When the weird and grotesque crime has been portrayed with sardonic wit, the blacks turn on their white-masked judges and condemn them to death. The play ends with all the Negroes dancing around a white-draped catafalque to the opening measures of the minuet from Mozart's *Don Giovanni*.

There have been other books written on the subject of prejudice and discrimination, but none in which the white race is pitted so shamefully against the black. Jean-Paul Sartre's *The Respectful Prostitute* deals with the duplicity of a Southern senator with regard to a prostitute. The senator wants her to perjure herself to protect his nephew, who has killed a Negro. The girl sells her body, and she sorrowfully sells her soul; but the senator has no integrity of soul whatever. This is a powerful story with striking moral protest, but unlike *The Blacks* it could be told of people regardless of their color. *The Blacks* has universal dramatic significance too, but it is first and foremost a chilling cry against the cant of white supremacy.

Political protest has also found a ready hearing in modern literature. Arthur Koestler's *Darkness at Noon* is typical of the dilemma that is drawn between social structures that are free but irresponsible and political orders that are publicly concerned but personally tyrannical.

Perhaps of greater significance than the literature of political partisanship, because it is more abiding, is the new probing of the psychological aspects of morality. Strindberg's play *The Father* is a superb example of how crime can be perpetrated psychologically by the deliberate breaking of a necessary personal relationship. *The*

*Father* is the story of an ordinary couple who have lived long years of unhappiness together. Like Aeschylus's Greek king Agamemnon, the Swedish captain is a victim of his wife's sex hatred and her lust for power. Laura, the wife, has a terrible femininity in which she exploits her husband's clumsy weakness. She is neither a bluestocking nor a virago in her femininity; she is simply an ordinary female who, lacking common sense, thinks she must dominate her husband. By planting the seed of nagging doubt about the paternity of her child, since it is true that a woman and a woman alone knows who is the father of her child — that is, she *can* know it although it is not true that she always *does* know it — Laura slowly and inevitably drives her husband mad. And by trickery she demonstrates that her wits are as strong as her will. She is just as guilty of murdering her husband as if she shot him in cold blood. She has him committed to a mental hospital on the strength of a letter he wrote to a doctor in which he admits his own madness. The moral protest for the emancipation of women is answered by this psychological protest that the dominance of women brings disaster.

The literature of protest, however, no matter what field it may probe, always rests on a commonly accepted moral foundation. It is taken for granted that the traditional code of conduct, based on an Aristotelian version of a biblical value system, is sufficient for the establishment of social justice and personal goodness. More recently a literature of revolt has developed in which these first principles themselves have been questioned. Protest calls for correction of conditions which violate accepted principles. Revolt rejects not only the conditions, but the principles also.

One of the early rebels in this primary revolt is Lady Chatterley in D. H. Lawrence's *Lady Chatterley's Lover*. She is fundamentally different from Emma Bovary and

all the shady ladies who preceded her. Madame Bovary
evokes sympathy as a heroine too, but only because she
is human and weak, as we are all human and weak. She
has strayed from marital chastity and has to be forgiven
as a sinner. Lady Chatterley asks for no forgiveness and
defies description as a sinner. She questions the morality
of morality itself. Morality denied her fulfillment as a
person. Only by shattering the whole concept of sin and
forgiveness, morality and righteousness, could she realize freely and fully what she could become. Under a
totally new aspect, a new morality, she could claim that
it was right for her to break loose from a foolish and re-
stricting fidelity to her husband since it was physically
impossible for him to satisfy her. According to this new
morality, the principle of keeping her troth in sickness
and in health had to be scuttled for a better principle
which would give her freedom to be herself.

A revolt of a different kind but nevertheless a revolt
against the old morality is the message Hugh Hefner
is proclaiming with his "Playboy Philosophy." Sex is
primarily a matter of pleasure not morality. It should
have no restrictions whatever so long as it is entered
into by consenting adults in the privacy of their cham-
bers. Any kind of relationship should be permitted —
homosexual, heterosexual, premarital, extra-marital —
so long as consent on all sides is given. Literature today
is filled with situations in which all these relationships
are explored with leering affirmation. The characters
are drawn with sympathy not in spite of the retributive
judgment that falls upon their aberrations. They are
drawn with sympathy because they defy the morality
that formerly judged them.

A highly respected example of the defiance of the new
morality may be found in Berthold Brecht's *The Life of
Galileo*. Galileo's researches ran counter to the Aristotelian astronomy which was supported by the church of

his day. His challenge incurred the wrath of the Inquisition even though the official Vatican astronomer confirmed his discoveries of the moons of Jupiter. When brought to trial and torture, however, Galileo recants and denies what he saw with his own eyes through his telescope.

These facts of history have always been viewed according to the old morality as a regrettable lapse of weakness on the part of a great man, yet possibly forgivable and understandable under the circumstances. Brecht interprets them in a new light. To challenge the traditional physics and remove the difference between heaven and earth, to put man in place of God — this is one achievement, and Galileo is to be celebrated for it. But to recant, to lie, so as to be able to continue working for the cause of science, and thus later produce the laws of motion—this is another achievement, an achievement in ethics which is as great as the one in physics. Here we have the birth of situation ethics, according to which the conditions of Galileo's time, together with his talent, produce a situation in which lying is better than truth. Again no forgiveness is asked because no sin has been committed. The lie is celebrated.

The new morality is not unprincipled libertinism, however. Situation ethics is not antinomian. Jean-Paul Sartre's *Dirty Hands* shows how a man will kill for a cause with reluctance, but when he finds himself killing for the wrong reason, he will be conscience-stricken until he sets it right by sacrificing himself. The old morality about killing as a breach of the fifth commandment is no longer an issue. Killing is justified if it is needed to serve the cause of the party. Hugo in Sartre's play is a proletarian party worker in Illyria, an imaginary country in central Europe at the close of World War II. He is sent by his party to kill the party leader, Hoederer, because Hoederer has deviated from party policy by advocating a coalition with the army. Hugo is slow to do his job. Killing is a nasty business in which one's hands get dirty. After several false attempts, he is finally prodded into action when he discovers his wife trying to seduce Hoederer. In sudden jealous rage Hugo kills him. He thus does what his party ordered, but he does it for the wrong reason.

While he is in prison serving a sentence for his crime, it becomes evident to the central authority of the party that what Hoederer had advocated was expedient after all. Hoederer now becomes a hero after his death and Hugo becomes a villainous assassin who must be extirpated by the party after his release from prison. Thus as the situation changes, the definition of justice changes. But Sartre has something more to say. Hugo has suffered during his prison years because he has always known that he killed out of selfish passion and not for the cause. Thus when he is released and has the opportunity to escape through the favors of a girl friend, he chooses rather to give himself up when the party members come to kill him. He proves to be an old-fashioned rebel in Camus' sense, and not a real nihilistic revolutionary. He is willing to sacrifice himself for his rebellion. He has a just cause for which he will die. The true Communist today will not do this. He will change his policy without reason. He will get dirty hands without compunction. He has no conscience and no innocence other than his success.

The new morality is an ethic of personal integrity. No code of justice, nor any situation, may violate the freedom of the individual to be himself, yet the individual is not without responsibility either, and he must weigh this responsibility in every situation against his personal integrity.

There is a newness in this existential morality, but basically it is only part of an old story. It is new in that it revolts against the systematic absolutism of the Victorian period. The revolt of Jesus when he said that the sabbath was made for man and not man for the sabbath was an affirmation of the integrity of the person in the ambiguity of his situation. The stand which Paul made against the Judaizers on the one hand and the gnostic antinomians on the other shows that the Christian position is not merely a revolt, however. The quest for holiness probes deeper and reaches higher than either protest or revolt. This quest grasps at reality as reality struggles from age to age with the false dilemma between absolutism and relativism in morality. There is always a new revolt against legalism because there is always an old legalism; but then the newfound freedom becomes an unfettered license and it produces a counterrevolution of absolutism.

Man's search for goodness, when it is seen in the vacillations of history and more profoundly in the life of the cosmic story, reveals a basic ambiguity in the core of reality. This ambiguity poses superficially as a dilemma between absolutism and relativism, tempting people to choose between them according to their temperament. As in the case of most dilemmas, however, there is a third horn which is not readily seen unless we hear the voice of the Spirit and acknowledge both his precarious guidance and the fundamental reality of the ambiguity.

In the Christian view, man is caught up in a situation which has traditionally been called sin. In sin man does not have the crystal-clear choice between good and evil. There is a mass of perdition corrupting the whole world of which he is a part both as responsible agent and victim of superior forces. Man in sin finds that reality both crushes down upon him with oppressive heaviness and eludes him with evanescent airiness. We found this ambience of opaque solidity and fleeting fluidity to be man's curse in his search for love. It is no less so in his quest for holiness. The healing of holiness would seem to promise rest, but his search brings only torment and anguish because he is repeatedly torn between loves, between loyalties.

The recent American novel *Advise and Consent,* by Allen Drury, describes the sordid ambiguity of sin in the setting of Washington politics. The moving complexities of human intrigue and chicanery can be compared only with the swish and the swill of a sewer. This is the story of an able, aggressive, and idealistic senator from Utah who finds he must oppose the appointment of the President's nominee for secretary of state because he has information that the candidate early in his career had pro-Communist tendencies. Apart from this, the candidate has had a brilliant and impeccable career as a loyal statesman. Since the well-being of the nation depends on the direction of its foreign policy, no more important decision can come before the Senate. The variety of motives with which the senators enter into this decision is the complete description of sin. Party loyalty is scuttled in the bargaining for votes. Personal principles are sacrificed for party loyalty. Grand idealism is compromised for practical success. The plot becomes a web of conflicting threads, all crossing and tugging against each other. But the thread that breaks the web and brings the inevitable tragedy is the fact that the senator from Utah, Brigham Anderson, had had a homosexual interlude when he was a young man. His private sin comes back to haunt him just as he has haunted the President's nominee for his public sin. Under the threat of blackmail, he collapses and compounds the sin with suicide.

This is the picture of the ambiguity of sin in reality. No sentimental or grandiose loyalties to nation or family or ideals can whitewash the basic fact that all men grub in the dirt and none can cast the first stone.

Another American novel, a much earlier one, tells the

same story with none of the complicated cross-currents but with classic clarity and simplicity. Nathaniel Hawthorne's *The Scarlet Letter* is the story of how people in sin destroy themselves and others by their very pursuit of high principles. *The Scarlet Letter*, like *Advise and Consent*, is more the story of a community than of heroes and heroines. Hester Prynne, having been deserted by her husband, gives birth to a child by her minister, Arthur Dimmesdale, whom she refuses to expose in her trial. This is adultery and she is condemned by the community to wear the letter A over her breast as long as she lives. Her husband, Roger Chillingworth, returns, and without revealing himself to the community secretly preys upon the consciences of the pitiable lovers. Hester, whose confession and judgment were open, was pained but not broken. Arthur, whose guilt was kept in secret, nurtured a festering psychological cancer that destroyed him mentally and physically. Hawthorne pronounces his own moral at the end of the tale: "Be true! Be true! Be true! Show freely to the world, if not your worst, yet some trait whereby the worst may be inferred!"[3] Hawthorne felt, according to the Calvinist doctrine of public confession, that if Arthur Dimmesdale had openly acknowledged his sin he would have been healed. Hester grew strong under exposure to censure, but Arthur withered because he did not come clean. This may be true, although it is doubtful that any community would produce such a salvific effect since sin is more than the private quality of individuals. Since God alone heals, God alone must hear the confession. Yet this does not preclude the need for priestly intercession on the part of God's delegates. But running through the novel is a more pertinent thesis. It is the author's protest that the law breaks people when it is untempered with mercy. This is the underlying truth which *The*

[3] *The Scarlet Letter* (Heritage, New York, 1935), p. 276.

*Scarlet Letter* has in common with *Advise and Consent.* We are caught in the scandal of sin and condemned by the law of righteousness. Earnestly we pursue principles of purity so as to erase the stain of sin, but the more we strive the more we bring pain and destruction to ourselves and others. This is what Paul meant when he said the law increases sin. The Spirit gives life, but the letter kills.

Perhaps the most compelling character to illustrate man's monomaniacal quest for holiness is Ibsen's Brand. He is a Strelnikov maddened by religious purity. Brand is strong-willed and high-purposed, but he is also hard and demanding. His motto is "All or Nothing!" Morality for him is a matter of will. Not even sacrifice is enough if it is not willed. His flinty singularity was etched sharply against the fuzzy softness of his mother, his wife Agnes, the Baillie, and the Provost.

His mother is of clay, human clay, and he calls it dirt. She is weak, and greedy for money, even rummaging through her husband's pockets and his mattress on his death bed. She laments: "Why was my soul born in the flesh, if the love of the flesh is the death of the soul?" Because she will not give up her money, all of it, her son will not bring her communion before she dies.

His wife Agnes is human. With natural mother love she grieves the loss of her child. Brand tells her the boy's corpse is beneath the snow but that the child himself has been carried to heaven. She cannot separate the body from the child. Brand will not let her mourn and strips away even her memories. She clings to his baby clothes, but Brand tears them from her and gives them to a Gypsy. Agnes dies having made idols of the little things in life.

The Baillie and the Provost are pawns of officialdom. They serve the State with its compromise of principle for the sake of peace and security. Brand comes into his parish as a doer. He stirs the people from their sleep and gives them new life. The life he gives is not peace but struggle, yet it lifts them and they would have followed Brand to the moon. But Brand is not satisfied. He builds them a new church, but it is not great enough, so he locks the door and throws away the key. His goal is ever higher. "The church as it stands now," he says, "is small; to conceal this would be a lie." And the Baillie responds: "What is the good of calling a thing ugly. . . . The people are so perfectly satisfied, they think everything costlier and more perfect than anything they have ever seen before; do let them think so always!"[4]

The contemptible compromising and toadying of the Baillie and the Provost are matched by the fanatical willfulness of Brand. He drives himself higher and higher until finally the people can no longer follow. They are seduced by the Baillie's lie that they can all get rich quickly from a shoal of fish in the fjord. Brand is left with one follower, a Gypsy girl, and she is mad.

It becomes evident that in the deepest sense holiness is not legalistic conformity with the law as an absolute principle, nor is it the willful attempt to lift oneself by one's own bootstraps in a fanatical determination to do one's duty. While the weakness of all the other characters in *Brand* is not condoned, the wildness in Brand's demand for All or Nothing is nothing short of demonic.

We have said thus far that the new morality is not legalistic but situational. Positively it seeks to serve the integrity of the person. We have seen the beginnings of this notion in Hester Prynne and a full-blown blast of it in Brand. Hester regrets what she did, but she never repents. She wears her scarlet letter with pride and dignity because she accepts herself for what she is. It is not Hester who lacks holiness, it is the community that is

[4] *The Works of Henrik Ibsen* (Roslyn, N.Y.: Walter J. Black, 1928), p. 657.

sick. Brand is fanatical in his determination to fulfill his
will despite the law or public opinion, despite the drag
of natural desire or the lesser duties of family and community. But the tragedy of Brand does not evoke the
same sympathy as we feel for Hester Prynne. Holiness
is certainly not in the lethargy of the villagers, nor in the
earthy desires of Brand's mother, nor in the weak humanity of his wife, nor in the political compromise of the
Baillie and the Provost; but neither is it in the abandoned willfulness of Brand. He seeks with delirious
excitement to be himself, but the higher he goes on the
mountain toward the ice church, the more tragic he becomes.

Ionesco has said all this with tragicomic finesse in *Victims of Duty.* Now we have moved into the Theater of
the Absurd, where the ideas that were born in the earlier protest and revolt have come into full flower. With
Ionesco we do not merely protest moral deviation, nor
revolt against ethical principles; we challenge metaphysical structure. He does this with hilarious comedy
and ingenious theater. Ostensibly the play is an analysis
of drama itself. In a play about plays he says that all
drama from ancient Greece to the present has been a
thriller in which a detective lurks about so as to solve
the mystery in the last act. To illustrate this, he begins
his play with an average middle-class couple spending
a quiet evening at home. A detective comes to their door
to investigate a neighbor. He wants to know if Choubert,
the husband and hero of the play, knows whether his
neighbor spells his name with a "d" or a "t" — was it
Mallod or Mallot. At once the detective begins to cross-
examine Choubert, probing into his subconscious to discover hidden knowledge of the reality about Mallot, or
Mallod. The assumption is the Freudian myth that the
real self, the whole and healthy self, is subliminal, and
that we need only tear away the crust of repression to

get to the bottom of reality. As the detective peals away layer after layer of false personality, Choubert changes his identity. His view of his wife changes too, and she changes. First she becomes a seductive temptress, then an ancient crone, and then the willing mistress of the detective. Choubert goes down farther and farther through the sound and light barriers until he is beyond all reach, but instead of finding solid reality at the bottom of his being, he finds nothing. He returns to the stage as a child, and his wife is now his mother.

With this scorching parody of the Freudian myth, Ionesco does something far more shattering than exposing the fraudulence of Freud. He challenges the grand assumption of Western culture, the more basic Platonic myth that there is an identity of the person, that there is an irreducible reality in the human character. We have quarreled over the symptoms and the palliatives for the relief of the disease of man, but we have never before really questioned the diagnosis. Ionesco doubts that there is an integral personality that can be isolated for cure. When we go to the bottom of our being, we do not find a whole, real self; we find nothing. Ionesco repeats his message in the play by having the detective send Choubert up the Mont Blanc Massif and even higher into the wild blue yonder. Like Brand climbing to his ice church, Choubert mounts the snowy crag until he drifts away in evanescent nebulosity. Once more he ends in nothingness.

Ionesco seems to be challenging the Platonic and Aristotelian core of Western culture with the existentialism of Jean-Paul Sartre. The detective-psychoanalyst assumes that all mysteries can be solved, all diseases can be diagnosed. "As for me," he says, "I remain Aristotelianly logical, true to myself, faithful to my duty, and full of respect for my bosses."[5] Choubert, on the other hand,

[5] *Victims of Duty,* in *Plays,* Vol. II (New York: Grove), p. 159.

proves that the mystery cannot be solved, that people do not have a simple single identity, that we are, in Sartre's terms, always in process of becoming what we choose. Man is really nothing, he is "the being through which nothingness enters the world."[6]

The contention of the existentialists, with all their talk about being, nothing, becoming, and existence, is that man, unlike the material things of this world, is not a thing or an object. He is nothing in that he is no thing, not this thing or that thing that can be manipulated or exploited or disposed of. He is a subject who chooses to be what he is. This terrible freedom is both his glory and his tragedy, for with it he is God. Indeed this is precisely what Sartre has done: he has put man in the place of God. Whereas the old mystics, following Plato's analysis of Being and Nothing in the *Republic* (V, 477), gave the exalted place of Nothingness only to God, the atheistic Sartre follows the same line of reasoning and gives this place to man.

Ionesco seems to challenge, up to a point, the Platonic irreducibility of the human character and the Aristotelian logic of the unity of person, time, and place. What happens, however, to the quest for holiness as a quest for the integrity of the person? What if there is no person? If we are what we choose, who or what is to tell us what to become? At this point Ionesco seems to reverse himself and to parody the existentialists. A strange character named Nicholas d'Eu enters and kills the detective, thus releasing Choubert from his duty to search for his real self, all of which searching is comically devised to discover whether Mallod(t) is spelled with a "d" or a "t." Now the play should end with the triumph of release, but it does not. Instead, Choubert becomes a victim of duty all over again, with Nicholas d'Eu trying to

[6] Jean-Paul Sartre, *L'Etre et le Neant* (Paris: Gallimard, 1943), p. 60.

stuff up the hole in his consciousness with the bread of life, which is what the detective was doing before he was killed.

Ionesco thus says no to both Platonism and existentialism. He leaves us in the tragicomic situation of the clown, crying and laughing at ourselves at once. We are not self-identifiable persons. We cannot become ourselves simply by a serious application to our duty. Nor can we become ourselves by release from our duty, because we will always be victims. We are free to choose, but we do not have an absolute freedom, as God might. It is an adolescent wishfulness on the part of the existentialists to think that we have such freedom. For this reason the drama of Ionesco as story is infinitely closer to reality than is either Platonic or existentialist philosophy. The story is open ended because reality is not yet finished. Philosophy seeks resolution. There must be an end to the argument. It must come out either with a well-defined and irreducible person that can be labelled holy, or with a becoming subject who is free to choose holiness. The story of reality is that holiness can be neither sought nor willed. It is beyond our grasp because it is given.

# IV

## A Tale of Triumph and Hope

We have uncovered evidence to support the thesis that the literature of the world reveals a key to reality and that the common themes may be used as bridges between various cultures. We have found a common concern with the force of evil that leaves men everywhere anguished and possessed. We have seen men looking for love with a passion unquenchable despite the fact that it ends in unrequited tragedy. We have followed the febrile quest for holiness and found that goodness is a gift within this world and not a goal to be won through escape.

In all the stories that have explored these themes there is manifest another theme, the theme of conflict and victory, of hope and triumph. The stories say, "'Give us our dream!" The ancient pagan Oriental hopes are matched by the Medieval Christian dreams in the Arthurian romances. Modern literature, although surfeited with dismal doubt, is also replete with hesitant yearning. My contention is that all this is but a reflection of the fundamental hope in the triumph of the Messiah. There is in the great stories of mankind a hope that will not die, and this hope will find its realization in the story of Christ with his promise and fulfillment, both in the coming of Jesus and in his coming again at the last day.

Ancient Hindu epics tell of conflict and victory. The *Mahabharata* is a lengthy narrative of the bitter feud between members of an ancient royal family. The story is more than historical, because the gods enter into the battle much as they did in the story of the Trojan War. Thus while the conflict is seemingly coarse and trivial, it is actually the story of a cosmic struggle in which coarse and trivial people play a vital part. The *Ramayana* epic has even closer parallels with the story of the *Iliad*. Rama is one of two human incarnations of the preserver God Vishnu, the other human incarnation being Krishna. The stories told about Rama and Krishna are the most fascinating and popular in all Hindu mythology. The stories of creation and destruction, of beginnings and judgment, are centered around Brahma and Shiva in the Hindu triad, but Vishnu inspires tales of hope and redemption.

In the *Ramayana* epic, Vishnu and his wife Lakshmi become incarnate as Rama and Sita. Conflict arises when Sita is stolen from Rama and carried off to Ceylon by Ravana, the demon king of the Rakshasas. The abduction and battle which follow are similar in many respects to the story of Helen, who was carried off to Troy by Paris until the forces of the Greeks under Agamemnon, through the heroic and wrathful intercession of Achilles, were able to restore Helen to her husband Menelaus and bring them back to their kingdom of Sparta. When Sita is spirited away to Ceylon, Rama gathers the forces of the Nizams and Maharajas of India in hot pursuit. He is aided by the intercession of the monkey god, Hanuman, who commands thousands of monkeys to intertwine their tails and form a bridge over the straits of Ceylon.

This is the story of the hope that family fidelity, that filial, fraternal, and conjugal devotion, when broken, might be restored and preserved. It is the epic of the

establishment of a kingdom and a culture through conflict, based upon the sympathetic and humane loyalties
of the family. The narrative is developed along with the
historical conquest of the Dravidians by the Aryans as
they pushed southward to establish a common culture
throughout the subcontinent of India. The Trojan War
was a similar single raid, which came to epitomize the
entire conquest of the Mycenaean culture as it became
fully established on the Greek peninsula about 1200
B.C. The similarity in the narratives does not discount
the historicity of either tale. No doubt there was a conflict among the Greeks at Troy; no doubt there was a
similar pursuit of an abducted queen to the island of
Ceylon. But the two histories are remembered and recorded because they each enter into a story which is
greater than their history. Their histories tell a tale of
triumph in the face of a bitter enmity that would divide
families and pollute human affections. These histories
are worth telling because they recount how men have
been able to retain their humanity and rise above the
demonic divisiveness of animal passions so that they can
cultivate a benign civilization in which peace and beauty
and creativity can flourish.

Vishnu in the form of Krishna has inspired many other
cherished tales. The story of Krishna, which has evoked
the most excitement through the centuries, is celebrated
in the great festival of Dipavali. In the north of India,
village after village was destroyed by the marauding
evil monster Narakasura. He devoured people and cattle
alike with insatiable greed. Prayers were lifted to the
gods of Mount Meru for the deliverance of the people.
Vishnu, the compassionate preserver, answered their
supplications by incarnating himself in the form of
Krishna. As he prepared himself for battle, he took with
him, in addition to his great sword, a small bow, a single straight arrow, and his beloved, almond-eyed Satya-

bhamma, one of his sixteen thousand wives. On the desert sands Krishna engaged Narakasura in a fierce battle to the death. For fourteen days and fourteen nights they fought, raising such a cloud of dust that they blotted out the light of the sun and the moon. Fearful darkness more dense than a monsoon cloud spread over the land. Krishna had inflicted mortal wounds upon Narakasura, but the monster was slow to die, and suddenly in weariness Krishna fell in a swoon. He was about to be slain by the monster in a final burst of evil strength, but the lovely Satyabhamma quickly strung her husband's bow and sent the arrow straight to the heart of Narakasura. His body was placed on a bier and burned. The light of the fire now shone in the heavens more brightly than the sun and the moon had shone before. Ever after for fourteen days and fourteen nights, the festival of Dipavali, a feast of lights, brightens all India in celebration of Krishna's victory over the evil one.

This story of Krishna is very different from the epic tale of Rama. More like the story of St. George and the dragon, this tale has lost its specific connection with history, if it ever had one, and also it does not embrace the historical establishment of a culture. Yet it inspires as much devotion as the Rama story and reaches into the same basic human hope in victory over evil. The method of conquest is crude and the appeal is therefore primitive, but the story lives because it is part of the greater story of conflict which assaults people everywhere and because, regardless of how the victory is won, the hope in it is universal.

Pagan Oriental hope is by no means limited to this coarse conflict. Embedded in the *Mahabharata* is a book called the *Bhagavad-Gita, Song of the Celestial One,* which completely sublimates hope by lifting it above the action and inaction of this world into a tranquil heaven of changelessness. The story of this poem is about

a warrior prince, Arjuna, who finds himself caught in
battle with members of his own family — fathers and
grandfathers, sons and uncles, the familiar faces of those
he loves. He despairs of the fighting and throws away
his bow, saying: "I shall not strike them. Now let them
kill me, that will be better." Whereupon, Krishna, in the
guise of Arjuna's charioteer, speaks to him, smiling, "Your
words are wise, Arjuna, but your sorrow is for nothing.
The truly wise mourn neither for the living nor for the
dead." Krishna then outlines two paths of aspiration to
blessedness, one of meditation and the other of action.
Some are called to contemplate, and they reach tranquillity by the yoga or discipline of self-controlled
thought. Others are called to action, but their discipline
must be selfless, with no thought for the fruits of their
action. If they dwell upon the results of what they do,
they will end in misery. But if a warrior simply does his
duty and obeys his command without questioning what
will come of it, then he too, like the one who meditates,
will achieve tranquillity.

In both cases hope is sublimated beyond the pragmatic concerns of this life. One cannot be defeated if he
does not hope in this thing or that but rather lifts his
vision to the reality which is changeless and which is
ultimately nothing. If, however, one seeks by deliberate
nonaction to avoid a specific result, this selfish concern
will only bring misery, just as much as if he takes up an
action to gain a desired result.  Only by rising above
things and hoping in the reality of nothing (no thing),
can tranquillity be found. In the *Chandogya Upanishad*
the story of the education of Svetaketu is told. The boy
asks his father to instruct him in the essence of things.
"Be it so, my child," the father replies. "Fetch me thence
a fruit of the banyan tree."

"Here is one, sir."

"Break it."

"It is broken, sir."

"What do you see there?"

"These seeds, almost infinitesimal."

"Break one of them."

"It is broken, sir."

"What do you see there?"

"Not anything, sir."

The father says, "My son, that subtle essence which you do not perceive there, of that very essence this great banyan tree exists. Believe it, my son. That which is the subtle essence, in it all that exists has its self. It is the True. It is the Self, and thou, O Svetaketu, art it."

From the yoga of the *Gita* to the mysticism of the *Upanishad*, we have moved farther and farther away from the reality of story into a realm of nothingness. When it is said that the essence of banyan trees and little boys and all else in the world is nothing, we have left the excitement of life with its hopes and conflicts, its frustrations and triumphs. If hope comes to mean a discipline in which there is neither laughter nor tears, then the tranquillity of the mystic *me on* has lost its story. There is no place in it for animals, men, angels, or gods. There is only the eternal boredom of the void.

We have found this before in the themes of evil, love, and holiness. Each time evil or love or holiness is refined and spiritualized out of this world of matter, it becomes reduced to a deceptive nothing that is seductively attractive to those who weary of the conflict and lose hope in a tangible reality. The same progression may be observed in Medieval Christendom, where dream gradually became volatilized by romancers who first indulged in moralistic didacticism and finally slipped into mystic visions. The vitality of the original stories was lost because in their pious earnestness to convey the message or grasp the goal men forgot to tell the tale. My contention is that the story itself is reality, and once we try to get beyond

it with instruction or visions, we lose reality and sink
into some kind of reduced or perverted substitute in
which we are robbed of hope.

The Arthurian romances relate the Medieval Christian
dream as it played itself out in the Court of the Round
Table at Camelot. Here knights jousted with bravery
within the rules of courtesy and fair play. But they loved
with chivalry outside the marriage bond, and for this
illicit love the Round Table was finally broken apart,
first with the death of Arthur and then with the deaths
of Guinevere and Lancelot. It was the love of Lancelot
and Guinevere that shattered the dream which made
little Camelot an earthly symbol of the New Jerusalem.
Arthur was king and he gathered round him loyal
knights who were dedicated to search for the Holy
Grail. The Sangreal, as it was called, was the legendary
cup that Christ used at the Last Supper. According to
tradition, Joseph of Arimathea, who "begged the body
of Jesus" after the crucifixion, brought the cup to Glas-
tonbury, a town in Somerset, England. Having been
lost, the cup inspired for its recovery the greatest and
noblest exploits of bravery and valor among all the
knights in the service of King Arthur. Although Lancelot
was the most esteemed of all the knights, and although
he contributed most to the search, his love for Guinevere made it impossible for him to recover it or even to
see it, as did Percival and Bors. It was given to his son
Galahad to win the Grail and receive the beatific vision.

The Medieval dream was punctured by bigotry and
superstition. Much in real life was sordid and mean. At
the lower levels, the social structure became stagnant
with an inflexible serfdom and at the top, clumsy and
artificial, with knight errantry crusading for causes that
seemed holy but which were actually senseless. Yet the
dream was real and the hope was honest. Never before
or since have we heard this story told with such rapt at-

tention. Malory brought the legends together in the magnificent moral romance of *Le Morte Darthur,* Spenser attempted to recover them in *The Faerie Queene* with intolerably prolix allegory, and Tennyson returned to them with romantic nostalgia. Even today the stories live in the musical play *Camelot.*

The repetition of the theme is evidence that something genuine and real is carried by this plot. Men do hope for a kingdom of light in which there is honor, valor, respect, and nobility. It is not the hope or the dream that makes the quest ridiculous, but the quest did fail and it was laughed into oblivion by Cervantes in his comical satire *Don Quixote.* I suggest that the shift in Medieval hope from a real, storied struggle to a non-storied mystic vision brought the absurdity, and with it the collapse, of the culture. In important respects it was the same preoccupation with an etherealized nothingness that we found in the Neo-Platonic and Hindu weariness with this world. When the story becomes too real, men want to get out. They lose their dream because, fearing failure in any immediate quest, they project their hopes beyond this world to where they can never be tested. It was when the Medieval world became concerned with an otherworldly mysticism that their hope was lost.

The irony of history, however, is that the reversal of that concern, the shift in Renaissance humanism from otherworldliness to the pursuit of this-worldly values, has failed utterly to restore hope in the hearts of men. Today, with our total commitment to materialism, with our preoccupation with the affluence of things, we suffer from the same boredom as does the mystic in his realm of the void. One must search far among modern novels and plays to find statements of ultimate hope. There are no grand affirmations such as Dante produced in *The Divine Comedy* or Milton in *Paradise Regained.* The grim pessimism of our age is called realism. It is more like classic Greek tragedy than like the literature of any other period. So gloomy are the plays in the Theater of the Absurd that they have intentionally become comical, but their laughter is not healthy; it is more often hysterical and at best bitterly cynical.

Doubt is pervasive on the modern scene. With some authors doubt sinks to dark despair, but with a few there are glimmerings of a faint yearning, which if not yet hope is the abiding well from which hope springs. Of these we shall speak later, but now it is necessary to observe that the modern doubt has driven us to the same negations as did ancient pagan mysticism and Medieval mysticism. Doubt has been raised over accepted moral standards. Doubt has been raised over the unity of time and place and the integrity of persons. We have seen how Ionesco questioned personal identity in *Victims of Duty*. He does not present his case as a tragic search for lost identity, with the basic assumption that there is an identity to be found. He presents the skeptical doubt that there is an identity which individuals can call their own. When we search for this basic self, we find ourselves wandering from one self to another and ending in absolute vacuity. The hopelessness of hope, then, does not evoke tragic sympathy; it stirs risibility, but the laughter somehow leaves us with wounds rather than healing. Modern doubt leaves us in the same empty void of nothingness that believing mysticism found. Perhaps this objectivity, this sophisticated realism, this courageous rejection of pious wishfulness, is honest, but what do the rest of us do who have mysterious, unsought yearnings for more than final defeat? Is it less brave to renounce tranquillity for a struggle?

Wishfulness certainly leads to superstition and religiosity, but there is a genuine dream in all men to lift themselves above the animals, to build a city in which justice and freedom prevail, and finally to defeat death. This hope springs eternal and is ultimately expressed in the messianic promise of one who will come to establish such a kingdom on earth.

If our modern doubt makes such a hope dim today, it is nevertheless not dead. One example of yearning in the face of modern doubt is Tennessee Williams' play *The Glass Menagerie*. Unlike the plays of the Theater of Protest and Revolt and especially the Theater of the Absurd, this play belongs to a class of drama in which the sordid hopelessness of the human situation is recognized, but nevertheless a longing for release and redemption is expressed if not realized. Besides the plays of Tennessee Williams, we may cite the work of Arthur Miller, Thornton Wilder, T. S. Eliot, and much of Edward Albee as examples of messianic hope.

In *The Glass Menagerie* the yearning centers on the figure of a gentleman caller, whom Tom Wingfield refers to in the introduction to the play as a symbol for one whom we all hope will come to deliver us from our insufferable boredom. Tom is the son in a family that has lost its father and is wallowing aimlessly in a situation that is stifling and oppressive to everyone. Tom's life is shut in by his frightfully boring job as a clerk in a warehouse and by his nagging mother with her phony dreams about her glamorous girlhood. His only release is going to the movies and getting drunk. His sister Laura is crippled and pathetically shy. She is as fragile as the glass menagerie she has collected and cares for with sick devotion. Laura enrolled in a typing school but became so embarrassed because she could not keep up that she secretly quit and walked in the park every day instead of telling her mother. Laura's need arouses the quest for a savior. Amanda Wingfield, the mother, is an interminable babbler who has high ambitions for her children. To save her daughter, she asks Tom to bring home a gentleman caller. When he tells her one is coming, the peak of excitement is reached in the play. Frantic preparations are made. The house is spruced up, a feast is cooked, candles are lit, and Amanda puts on an old frock which she wore when she was a Southern belle. When the caller comes he is Jim O'Connor, an old high school classmate of Laura's. He had had the lead in the high school operetta *The Pirates of Penzance* and was expected to go far, but now he was only a warehouse clerk like Tom. All are disappointed, and the evening turns into a fiasco. Jim, however, is full of life and hope for himself and he tries his best to bring Laura out of herself, but he succeeds only in smashing one of her glass animals. He is already engaged to another girl and so when the reason for his invitation is exposed he leaves early.

The play ends in tragedy. Laura sinks more deeply into herself, Tom leaves home to escape the screaming and nagging of his mother, and Amanda Wingfield is left alone to nurse her defeated ambitions. It must not be thought that the gentleman caller is a messiah figure in any allegorical sense. The play is not an allegory. But it does say that people in the sordid slough of selfish loneliness long for someone to come to deliver them. The preparations they make for deliverance, however sincere, are always inappropriate to the point of being comical. The savior they desire is never the savior they get. When he comes, they reject him and he is unable to deliver them. Yet the possibility is there and the yearning is there. The tragedy is in the failure of bringing together the yearning and the possibility. This is the messianic story. It is not sentimental, because it does not wishfully tell a false tale of sweet success in the coming of the deliverer. The truth of reality is that the savior is not what we expect and is rejected when he comes. Yet the truth of reality is also that he comes. That we miss him is our tragedy. That he does not fit our expectation and supply what we want does not mean that he cannot bring us what we need. Our preparations for his coming are pathetic, raising every valley, lowering every hill, smoothing the way for him and striving in our heart of hearts to be good enough to merit his presence. But when he comes, our disappointment and fickleness combine to destroy him. Yet he promises to come again, and the story of human hope will not die.

The realist says such hope is impossible. It projects us into the realm of fantasy. We must guard against being deluded by wishful fantasy. Yes, but we are saying that fantasy is not to be opposed to reality, as nothing is opposed to something. We are saying that the world is a house of many rooms. The furniture of the room of actuality may be set in order or it may be upset. When it is upset, we do not say it does not exist. Likewise the furniture in the room of fantasy may be helpfully and healthfully arranged or it may be topsy-turvy. It is, of course, always surprisingly different from the furniture of actuality. But this difference does not make it nonexistent. It makes it non-actual, that is nonsensory, but reality may include both the actual and the illusory. This is the reason why story is so significant in the apprehension of reality. The play itself is an illusion. Drama is the art of the impossible. We see reality not in actuality but in the illusion of a stage. Hope that is centered in the impossible, that is nurtured by fantasy, is not necessarily wishful nor unreal. It may be falsely grounded when it is directed to fantasy, but it may be equally falsely grounded when it is directed to the actual. Hope that is healthy, hope that is holy, must rest in the real wherever this reality arises. In the messianic hope it arises from the inscrutable mind of God, whose ineffable speech is truly fantastic.

The inclusion of fantasy as a part of reality is mar-

velously portrayed in the musical play *Man of La Mancha* by Dale Wasserman. Instead of being opposed to
reality, fantasy in *Man of La Mancha* is necessary to
life for health and edification. The impossible dream of
Wasserman's Don Quixote lifts him, his friends, and his
enemies to a higher humanity. The virtues he pursues —
bravery, nobility, courage, gentleness — produce in him
and others a better life. Without the dream, we are left
in the sewer of lust instead of the clear stream of love.
Without the projected fantasy, we are tempted to settle
for a reality that is limited by sordid actuality. It is better to see, with the eye of illusory vision, not just what
actually is but also what ought to be. Only such a wonderfully imaginary vision can lift us above what we are.

Don Quixote sees in Aldonza, a bar wench, the fair
and virtuous Dulcinea whose beauty is beyond compar-
ison. Aldonza is actually an ugly peasant girl with a
broad face, a flat nose, coarse skin, and a large mole on
her lip with eight long, red whiskers. Moreover, she
smells of garlic and has no morals. Quixote sees her not as
she actually is but as she is in his dreams. He treats her
therefore as a fair princess. He swoons before her charm
and pledges himself to guard her honor.

But notice the difference between Wasserman's *Man
of La Mancha* and Cervantes' *Don Quixote*. The original Don Quixote is an antihero who loses faith in
his ideal chivalric code and dies a practical, faithless,
modern man. He had striven beyond human limits and
failed. His tragedy was a kind of *hybris* in which he
stretched himself foolishly and comically for an outworn
ideal that never had any sense. He ends in apathy, sorrowfully accepting the inevitable compromise with the
practical. Quixote's comedy is the incongruity of his
ideal in the face of actual facts. We are told by Cervantes that we must live within the realm of fact and hope
only in the hopeful. Quixote's ridiculous absurdity was

that he hoped in the hopeless. When we try to preserve the ideals of knight-errantry in the modern world — honor, bravery, service to the poor and weak — we only make fools of ourselves.

According to Cervantes' satire, the only morality is the new morality begun by Galileo, the true hero of the modern man, as he is portrayed by Berthold Brecht in the play we have already discussed, *The Life of Galileo.* When Galileo was asked to defend himself, he chose to lie in order to save his life. Lying is permitted if the situation demands, and Galileo's dishonesty is not excused as a forgivable weakness but is celebrated as a contribution to ethics as great as his discoveries in physics. This is the message of the modern myth, with proponents from Cervantes and Galileo to Sartre and Camus. All agree that the practical and concrete is the only reality, and that we must learn to live within it. To accept the facts is the only commandment; to wish for more is unsophisticated absurdity.

But *La Mancha* is quite different. Here Don Quixote says that facts are the enemy of truth! Wasserman's hero is really a hero. He is celebrated for his heroic pursuit of his illusory ideal. He is not the ridiculous foil of satire; he is the gleaming rapier of an ideal. He is presented to the audience as the one who is right when all the world is wrong. Cervantes' Don Quixote was laughably wrong and the world was right. Maybe Cervantes had enough sympathy for his antihero to think sadly of the incongruity between the pitiful knight and the world, but he certainly thought the incongruity was both real and irreconcilable. And between the two we would have to choose the world, because its actuality would persist while the wild dream of Quixote would only blow away.

In *La Mancha*, however, the world is wrong, sadly so but really so, and Quixote is triumphantly right, deliriously right. His madness is his salvation, and could be the salvation of the world. If only the world could be so mad! This is what the play sings. The truth was spoken even by Cervantes himself, although against his own book, when finally Senor Samson Carrasco, masquerading as the knight of the White Moon, brings Quixote down in ignominious defeat and forces him to give up his idiotic knight-errantry. When this happens, Don Antonio, a townsman, says: "O sir, what have you to answer for in robbing the world of so diverting a madman?"[1] For this reason, when in the musical play Don Quixote is tempted to doubt his dream on his death bed, he is wonderfully surprised by the visit of Aldonza, for he finds that she really is Dulcinea. She has been lifted by his dream, and even though he himself may forsake it, she knows she has been changed and she will not let him deny her or himself. The quest for an impossible dream, however, must never be taken for sentimental idealism. It is rather a highly realistic adventure deep into the mysteries of reality where facts and fantasies enrich each other in the excitement of conflict and triumph.

But you may ask, Is this not impossible for most of us? Who can follow a madman when the world wants to be sane? And who can believe in fairy stories when we are no longer children? With utmost clarity we must say that not all are called to believe. While we insist that Christ died for all, and there is no exclusiveness in the Christian faith, yet not all are given the gift of faith. But for those who have been called to believe, it is evident that unless they become as children they cannot enter the kingdom. With the wonder of the child, the impossible dream is the only reality for the messianic hope.

Perhaps in view of this need to become as children, it will not be misunderstood, although the terrible risk is

[1] *Don Quixote de La Mancha* (New York: Washington Square), p. 416.

recognized, if we close this discussion on the messianic hope with a reference to a certain fairy tale for children. Some of the risk may be lessened when it is reported that no less a person than C. S. Lewis is the author of the fairy tale. I refer to *The Lion, the Witch and the Wardrobe*, which is the first book in a series of seven called *The Chronicles of Narnia*. These are stories written for children, yet they have an equal fascination for adults, much as the tales of Tolkien inversely were written as fairy stories for adults but have completely entranced young readers.

C. S. Lewis borrows a device from Lewis Carroll and imagines four children tumbling through a wardrobe into the weird land of Narnia, a country all covered with snow and where it is winter all the time, but where Christmas never comes because it is under the spell of a wicked white Witch. The inhabitants of this land are fauns, satyrs, giants, dwarfs, naiads, dryads, and talking animals. Even the trees whisper and listen to conversations. The land and its people are strange, wild beyond imagination, yet we know it is real because the adventures described are completely probable in their surprising intrigue, and the characters, animal and fanciful, reflect our nature, the only nature we know. The story is the struggle of the lion, Aslan, to release Narnia from the magic spell of the white Witch. The magnificent and mysterious Aslan comes on an ancient promise when the children and all the enslaved creatures are engaged in a mighty battle with the forces of the white Witch. One of the children, Edmund, out of spite, jealousy, and sheer perversity, proves to be a traitor, however, and he falls freely but securely into the enticing trap of the Witch. Because of the malice of her magic spell and the childish rage of his rebellion, the curse of Adam descends upon poor Edmund, and in accord with the Emperor's Law, the traitor's blood must be given to the Witch. But there is a deep magic which says that another may pay this price, and Aslan comes to do just this, to the horror and uncomprehending sadness of the loyal children. It seems that all is lost when the lion is killed by the Witch and her wicked Wraiths, Hags, Horrors, Orknies, and Wooses. Aslan gave Narnia to the Witch, lost his own life, and did not save Edmund.

But there was a deeper magic from before the dawn of time which the Witch did not know. If a willing victim who had committed no treachery was killed in a traitor's stead, the table of his sacrifice would crack and death itself would start working backwards. Now Aslan roared with new life, Edmund returned to his senses and broke the Witch's wand, and crocuses began to poke their heads above the snow as Spring burst upon the land of Narnia.

The tale in its bare bones, stripped of its quivering flesh, is the Messiah's story, but Lewis tells it again with fresh imagery in the language of children. Authenticity rings through it with such power that one cannot put it down without saying Amen, this is most certainly true. The story of the anguished and possessed, the search for love and holiness, and the ultimate vector of meaning are all bound up in the hope and triumph which come by the lion Aslan.

# V

## The Search for Meaning

Any survey of literature will reveal major systems of meaning corresponding to the different cultures in world history. Variations in these systems of meaning account for the changing epochs in cultures. The variations may have multiple causes, although one primary reason seems to be cross-fertilization due to great migrations such as occurred in the Aegean region between the Dorians and the Achaeans, and in the Indian subcontinent between the Aryans and the Dravidians. But the basic reason for the rise of a culture is the peculiar vision of reality which the men of that culture develop. Christopher Dawson has said that the shift from animal existence to human civilization did not really occur with the invention of tools and weapons, as the Promethean myth claims. It occurred when men conceived a vision of reality, and this is fundamentally a matter of religious meaning. Religious vision produced ancient Babylon and Egypt. A new conception of reality occurred around the world in the sixth century B.C. and produced the Greek philosophers, the Jewish prophets, Gautama, and Confucius. This conception brought law and the ideal abstractions of Goodness, Truth, and Beauty. The intellectual rationalization of the culture, however, came late as a thoughtful explanation of what went before. First came the re-

164

ligious vision, then the aesthetic expression of it, then the ethical emulation of it, and finally the philosophical rationalization as explanation and apology. Thus religion and art show the vital intention of a living culture; philosophy is the last development. Dawson says: "The Greek statue must be first conceived, then lived, then made, and last of all thought."[1]

In ancient times the major system of meaning in Western culture was the Platonic-Aristotelian hierarchy of beings, with reality conceived as an ideal that is basically good and rational. Ideal reality is opposed by the nonbeing of evil, together with the nonbeing or mere becoming of illusory appearance. Such a view of reality sets in motion a drama of sorts. Goodness becomes the goal. Meaning requires a search in which there is a moral struggle in which failure is a real tragedy, but a tragedy that is always buoyed up by faith and hope that goodness will ultimately prevail and triumph over evil, that being will ultimately survive against nonbeing, that reality will ultimately abide in the face of transient, illusory appearance. This system of meaning set the stage in later Western culture for our plays and gave plot to our novels. It was not the only system of meaning in the West, however, as we shall see. The Christian revelation brought a view of the reality of time that has given direction as well as shape to history.

In the Orient a mystical system of meaning developed. The nonbeing of all things was affirmed. Nothing is more real than nothing. In a system which declares the reality of nothing, neither good nor evil is real, and hence there is no moral struggle. This accounts for the dearth of literary creativity and, indeed, the cultural stagnation of the East. Whatever struggle there is in the Eastern consciousness is a discipline to achieve tranquillity. Since

[1] *The Dynamics of World History* (New York: Sheed and Ward, 1956), p. 102.

this involves no antagonism between persons or situations, the only drama is a psychological nonaction in which the vibrant elements of story vanish. While in the West stories could be told of the conflict between good and evil, in the East the mystical smudge blurred the distinction. While in the West meaning was found in a reality worth striving for, in the East meaning was found in the tranquillity of not striving. If it makes no difference whether you act or do not act, so long as you do not strive to act or not to act, you cannot have a story. You may present a play and carry it off if you have great ingenuity, and if you also say some things of protest that may need to be said, but your drama does not tell a story. This is precisely what is being done today in the Theater of the Absurd, especially by Samuel Beckett and Eugene Ionesco, where Western ontology as well as axiology is attacked in the name of mystical nihilism.

It is interesting to notice that, while the two systems of meaning are fundamentally opposed, as optimism opposes pessimism and something opposes nothing, nevertheless they are alike in their negation of time. Platonism denies the reality of time in favor of abstract, ideational principles. Oriental mysticism dismisses time for its psychological vision. In both cultures the refusal to take time seriously and recognize its reality presents a hindrance to the telling of stories, since stories begin "once upon a time" and move through a progression of time to a climax. This obstacle prevails only in sophisticated circles, however, because primitive folklore has kept alive the stories of the gods with a naive realism.

In the West, however, another reason has kept storytelling alive, and this is a reason that may provide a bridge between the two cultures. The Judeo-Christian revelation of reality has provided Western culture with a view of time that is neither Platonic nor mystical. Judaism and Christianity are both messianic and eschatological. They both look in faithful hope for the coming of Christ to deliver the world from its sickness unto death. His coming will bring the endtime, not the end of time, but the time of the end. Judaism and Christianity differ only in their reading of the timetable, not in their view of time. Judaism looks for the coming of deliverance in the future. Christianity proclaims that deliverance has already come in Jesus of Nazareth, who arose from the dead to reign in heaven and earth. We are now living in the endtime; the fulness of time has come, the season of climax in God's story is now in progress. We can look for the last day with confidence since we have the sacrament of Christ's triumphant resurrection in baptismal regeneration and eucharistic renewal.

This is an exciting story. The eschatological view takes time seriously. A real progression is affirmed through conflict to a climax. Meaning is found in all the elements of story. There is genuine freedom of action. The action is cosmic in scope, not narrowed, not limited even to the historical, and certainly not reduced to a psychological argument within the human mind. All the elements of story which we have found to be the touchstone of reality may be found with superabundant meaning in the story of Christ. Because of this story we know that reality has meaning. We know that this meaning is rich in realms of actuality and realms of illusion. Sickness, as well as health, may be found in both actuality and illusion because there is a deceiver who seeks possession of all reality. Under his temptation we are anguished, and the situation we find ourselves in is fraught with both the irony and the humor of the absurd. Yet, in spite of demonic possession there is progress and growth in this world. The story moves on in time, and there is real change through conflict. The tragedy of our subjection is countered by the victory of our release. It is this messianic deliverance, and not any reasoned structure of values, that gives meaning to the moral struggle. Holiness in the Christian story is appreciated as a gift, not as a reward for virtue.

This abundantly rich story, etched in the hearts of all men alike through the universal hope in a meaningful deliverance from evil and death, but finally told in the manifold revelation of the New Testament, has become the source of meaning in every story that is told after it. Along with the Platonic value system, the Christian story has also produced plots for dramas and novels in Western culture. Indeed it is the Christian story that has given meaning to history itself. Instead of viewing time as the rotation of epochs as they are determined by the periods of the stars, Christians view history as itself a progressive story, part of the cosmic drama which is being authored by the mysterious mind of God. Its meaning is not nothing as it would be if all happened by chance, nor is it nothing as it would be if all were determined by fate. History has meaning because it has a part to play in the story, an important part, but not the whole part. That the story of history is told is due to the Christian revelation. How the story is told depends upon the degree of understanding and appreciation of the Christian revelation.

Ultimate meaning is sought, therefore, in terms of our personal identity as this identity finds its place in the historic stream of things, and as this historic vector in turn finds its place in the cosmic drama.

In our earlier discussion, particularly concerning the problem of pain and evil, we said much about the search for meaning as an attempt to recover lost identity. In the Requiem of Arthur Miller's *Death of a Salesman,* Biff Loman stands over his father's grave after the suicide, and with tearless despair he mutters: "He had the wrong dreams. All, all wrong. . . . He never knew who he was."[2] We search for ourselves in our dreams. Willy Loman dreamed of being well liked. This was the mark of success for him. But the meaning of a man's life must be more than the shell of other people's opinion. He must have an integrity in himself. Otherwise, when all the others go away there is nothing left but a void.

The integrity of the person as the mark of meaning is explored with bloodcurdling wit and rapier humor in Harold Pinter's play *The Homecoming*. This is the story of a philosophy professor who, after six years of teaching in America, brings his wife back to London to visit his widowed father, his uncle, and his two younger brothers. The house they live in is cold and bare, having had no woman in it for years. The father is losing his grip in the home. Crumbling authority is matched by the breakdown of meaning in the use of words by the two generations. One son, Lenny, is a pimp, whose aim in life is to exploit people. Another son, Joey, is a witless boxer whose animal passions make him act more like a chimpanzee than a champion. The professor, Teddy, is detached. He has the objective self-awareness of sophistication. While the others simply act without consciousness of their action, he stands aloof and watches with contempt. The others act to satisfy their immediate human needs. The only meaning they require is the service of their gluttony. The audience is invited, as it were, to observe with the professor the unmasking of human existence as a woman is brought into the house of men. The sudden deterioration is so shocking and unnameable that the fragile and prudish bachelor uncle collapses with a heart attack. The father and brothers, however, with natural ease contrive a situation in which Teddy's wife, Ruth, is invited to stay on and not return with her husband to her three little sons. She is asked to do housework for the father, become a part-time prostitute for

[2]*Death of a Salesman* (New York: Viking, 1949), p. 138.

Lenny in his stable of whores, and a lover for Joey. Ruth slides into this arrangement with deadpan feline slipperiness, while her husband acquiesces inexplicably.

Perhaps there is a mythical symbolism in the coming of the young woman to replace the dead mother, who had been a promiscuous bitch. Teddy may have married Ruth because she was the image of his mother, and when he brought her home this sluttishness was released under the provocation of his father and brothers. Each was looking for love in his own way, and the woman with her supple grace was pliable enough to be used in every way. But here is the great ambiguity of the play. As soon as it is all agreed that she shall stay on, the terrible doubt is raised as to who uses whom in the battle between the sexes. After slobbering over her and begging for a kiss, the father cries out in stark horror, "She'll use us, she'll make use of us, I can tell you! I can smell it!" Is this the meaning of unmasked existence? Do we use one another only to awaken to the tragedy that we are being used? Raped integrity is the tragedy of mutual exploitation.

Rapacious tearing at the vitals of our personal integrity is exceeded only by the loss of integrity itself through the removal brought by death. When we probe this enigma, we reach into a mystery that is as alluring as it is dark. Perhaps we can never know the meaning of life until we know the meaning of death. There are many kinds of death. There may be many meanings, there may be none, but men will always be haunted by a protest within their breasts against death's silent and chilling thievery. Like Zorba the Greek, after the young widow was stoned and stabbed by her villagers, they ask with pained and uncomprehending dismay: "Why do the young die? Why does anybody die? Tell me." His intellectual friend answers with honest simplicity, "I don't know." Then the earthy Zorba charges at him with indignant rage, "What's the use of all your damn books? If they don't tell you that, what the hell do they tell you?" And then comes the sorrowful response of sophistication, "They tell me about the agony of men who can't answer questions like yours." The sensitivity of the truly human person is that he not only feels every pain of life and its loss, but he also has the infinite anguish of knowing his pain. As we rise in our humanity above the brutes, the depth of meaning increases, but by the same token the void in meaning expands, and this is the measure of our pain.

At the point of death, more poignantly than at any other time except possibly at birth, men are compelled to search for meaning beyond themselves. For this reason, I submit, all attempts to settle upon personal integrity and the recovery of personal identity are ultimately shallow, because no man is an island. It is not my right to be myself that makes for meaning. It is my obligation to others that gives sense and direction to my life. When I think in terms of rights, I end by isolating and insulating myself until I find myself in Sartre's hell, the room with no exit. But when I think in terms of obligations, I move out from myself in a never-ending adventure embracing all history and the story beyond.

We have observed that *Dr. Zhivago* is not only a love story, but also a man's struggle for meaning in a chaotic world of convulsive change. Beyond him and above him and behind him is the sweep of history. Where is it all going? How can he find his little niche? Why can't he work and love without being swept by its fierce currents? These are questions that can be asked only in a Christian context. They have no meaning in a Platonic or Oriental system of thought. As we ask the meaning of men for each other, we move under the shadow of the cross and we increase our pain rather than soothe it. As deeper and broader questions are asked, meaning is built up even though the agony is increased and the answers are not given.

The tranquillity of Zen, which seeks desperately to avoid pain, may be attractive, but it is bought at the expense of a stagnating culture in which individuals may dream but millions of the masses starve. Our maddening machines, which are with all science a fruit of Christian materialism, are a threat to our humanity and all personal sensitivity, but they also make us free and powerful and rich. They create social change in which we all become participants in the creation of a new world. Historical progress means that men may live and die for the development, and literally the evolution, of a brave new world. The uniformity of nature with its repeatable processes is transcended by the unidirectional thrust of history with its unrepeatable freedom. To share in this creation brings the meaning of joy and satisfaction, and beyond this there is the meaning of obligation and responsibility for the new power that is placed in our hands.

Meaning is therefore built up, and our problem is increased, as we sense the need to find a place for ourselves beyond nature within history, and beyond history within the cosmic story. Although at first the staginess of Thornton Wilder's *Our Town* was considered ingenious by the critics, and although its sentimentalism is still popular at the box office, the true profundity of the play is its grasp of the place of individuals and a community in the cosmic sweep of things. Wilder says in his preface to *Our Town*:

> The recurrent words in this play (few have noticed it) are "hundreds," "thousands," and "millions." Emily's joys and griefs, her algebra lessons and her birthday presents — what are they when we consider all the billions of girls who have lived, who are living, and who will live? Each

individual's assertion to an absolute reality can only be inner, very inner.[3]

Emily expresses the message of the play when she says that we do not appreciate life until death takes it away. It is really the living who are dead, and only the dead who know what it means to live. In the last act Emily dies and goes to her grave. She now knows the full meaning of life, but she is still reluctant to leave the living. She is allowed to return one day to relive her twelfth birthday. It only makes her sad, however, because she knows now what the living do not know. She knows the joy of life, and it hurts her to see how nobody sees anybody else, nobody really talks to anybody. Everyone is securely encapsulated in his own complacency, narrowed to an existence that is little when it could be infinite.

Grover's Corners is a type of all the world. It has its place in nature, as the professor relates at the beginning: "Grover's Corners lies on the old Pleistocene granite of the Appalachian range. I may say it's some of the oldest land in the world."[4] Its history is marked by the gravestones in the churchyard and by the daily reports in the *Sentinel*. The editor, Mr. Webb, tells the sociological facts of the census, the percentage of Republicans and Democrats, Protestants and Catholics, all the vital statistics in the community. A clue to its cosmic meaning is given by the little sister of George Gibbs when she tells George about a letter her girl friend received from her minister addressed to her at "Grover's Corners; Sutton County; New Hampshire; United States of America; Continent of North America; Western Hemisphere; the Earth; the Solar System; the Universe; the Mind of God." "And the postman brought it just the same!" Here

[3] *Three Plays* (New York: Harper, 1957), p. xii.
[4] *Ibid.*, p. 21.

we see a child growing up to an awareness of her own meaning in the world. She is someone, with a particular place and time, and ultimately she is someone in the mind of God.

In order to find place and meaning for persons we must therefore establish the meaning of history in the cosmic story. To have meaning, history must move to a goal. The New Testament writers all recognized this and expressed it in terms of the second coming of Christ with the final resurrection and judgment of the world. This is not the end of time but the endtime when all things will be made new. Tertullian saw the need for this eschatological thrust in the meaning of history, but he took his apocalyptic millenarianism so literally that the reality of the story vanished in the proclaiming of the principle. Ironically the very thing the Christian Gospel affirms most heartily, the reality of time, was lost in Tertullian's fundamentalist sentimentalism. Preachment and moralism replace narrative and parable in such a system, and history succumbs to meaninglessness in the preoccupation with futurism.

Origen followed another tack, sailing on the winds of Plato's idealism. He likewise relegated time and history to the background when he reached for eternity by means of the allegory. Meaning was sought beyond this "bank and shoal of time," not in the futurist fundamentalism of Tertullian, but in a nontemporal goal of eternity. Lugubrious attachment to the natural, the concrete, and the particular in the nineteenth century brought a furious reaction by writers like Proust, Woolf, Joyce, and Faulkner in the direction of this Origenistic and Platonic understanding of timelessness. Revolt against attention to the here and now derived from the complaint that such preoccupation was both trivial and deceptive. Meaning must be found in reality, and since the concretions of history are broken, reality must be above history in the timeless ideal.

The plaint of Samuel Beckett, who gets his inspiration chiefly from James Joyce, is given in graphic terms in *Happy Days*. In the first act, Winnie, the heroine, is buried up to her waist in a mound of sand. In the second act she is buried up to her neck. Throughout the play she has only her handbag to rummage through and a shiny pistol to fondle. Her old husband says practically nothing because she chatters all the time. He tries to climb the mound to reach his wife, but at the play's end he has not come close, and it is not sure whether he has been trying to grab the revolver to kill his wife, or to kill himself, or to take it away so he can kiss his wife. The message is as blatant as Grand Opera that women are buried up to their necks in trivia and their husbands cannot get close to them, or even get a word in edgewise.

Beckett repeatedly has his characters say that they can do nothing about the circumstances of their lives, which are always sordid, solitary, brutish, and mean. He then has them play with trivia like toothbrushes, hats, or boots, because these things help them pass the time of day, they tide them over. In all this, Beckett's wail and lament is bitter because he finds life to be fraudulent. If time is a cheat and a robber, Beckett is quick and eloquent in his assent, but unlike quiet mystics who have also wearied with this world, he has nothing but a strident blast of contempt and no hope for escape to serenity beyond. The only meaning is meaninglessness. Deliverance from time is no more possible for Beckett than the endurance of time. Happy days is a phrase one spits out like wormwood and gall.

It seems that all the possibilities have been tried. Meaning has been sought beyond history, within history, and above history. If injustice prevails and death cuts us down in time, a meaningful resolution is projected in an apocalyptic future at the end of time. But this has demonstrated a lack of social concern, and men still cry for meaning here and now. With fresh courage and strong will we turn to the task of building in the present, whether it be our personal lives, our nation, or a culture. We strive to make meaningful the immediate cause of our concern, but before long we find ourselves immersed in the senseless trivia that Beckett speaks about, with nothing, absolutely nothing, "fully guaranteed . . . genuine pure." Finally, if we cannot find abiding meaning beyond or within history, we look inward and above. We look for a sense of values that is always good and that we can grasp in the psychological present, neither in the unreachable future nor in the elusive and fleeting contemporary. This too becomes both barren and cruel because nothing is always good. Circumstances and persons vary and the definition of goodness varies with them. Time means change and growth. "New occasions teach new duties; Time makes ancient good uncouth."[5]

When we project our hopes into the fantasy of the future, we neglect the reality of the present and end in a nightmare of callous injustice. When we commit ourselves to the needs of the historical present, we soon become drowned in the fast flow of fashions, since meaning is sought only in what is new. And when we look with Proust for "deliverance from time" for an abiding meaning that is absolutely real, for some truth and beauty and goodness that will prevail, we soon find that any definition of such an absolute is either so abstract and lacking in content as to be sterile or so inflexible and inadequate as to be cruel in its application to particulars.

Are we left with the despair of Samuel Beckett? Another possibility remains when we consider that all three of these solutions to the problem of meaning are reduc-

[5] James Russell Lowell, "Once to Every Man and Nation."

tionist and simplistic. Without being eclectic, we can recognize that there are elements of truth in each. The error of each is that of every heresy in which a partial truth pretends to be the whole. The truth of Tertullian's eschatology is its future thrust which forces us to take time seriously. Already we see that a combination of eschatology and historicism is possible, if neither is allowed to swallow the other. This tension can be maintained if we recognize an absolute above both history and the eschaton. This is precisely the Christian message we find in Augustine, although it must be recognized that the form in which he put it is shaped largely by Platonism.

It is the Christian Gospel that introduces meaning into history. The deterioration after the fall is countered by the messianic promise. The coming of Jesus proclaims the fulfillment of this promise within history. History now moves with an ambiguous progression toward an endtime. The climax has come and we live now in the denouement. Christ is bringing all things into subjection under himself so as to turn them over to the Father at the last day (I Cor. 15:24). There is neither a simple evolutionary progress nor an inevitable devolution in history. We are confronted rather with an ambiguity in which conflict persists and even grows as we rise to higher and higher levels of community. The resolution of conflict, the ultimate victory, is therefore projected to the future, but because of Jesus it is proleptically evidenced in the past and the present. Part of this evidence is the mere history of Jesus' birth, life, death, and empty tomb. Add to this the mere history of the birth, life, suffering, and survival of the church as a human institution. In themselves these historical facts do not compel belief, nor do they carry any authoritative meaning. Jesus, for all this, may have been a great genius of passing significance. The church too may be said to have had its day. But there is a point of penetration which we may call the moment of faith, when the mere story of history meets a greater story. Something happened with Jesus, and continues to happen in the church, which is not empirical, nor rational, nor imaginary. The mystery of this happening is more real for those it strikes than dreams or sensible or rational experience, but it is given only to those who are chosen (Acts 10:41). Thus anyone could have seen the empty tomb, and anyone can see the bread and wine of the eucharist, but only with the gift of faith did the risen Jesus appear to some, and only with the gift of faith do the elect in the community of the church celebrate the eucharistic presence of Christ. It is because of this intersection of successive events in time with the mysterious story of Christ that history gets its meaning as an ambiguous progression. The several events within history become meaningful to the whole because the whole of history has a place in a larger story.

What does it mean to say there is an ambiguous progression of history? It means that a radically new hope entered into the hearts of men when, with the Christian revelation, time was taken to be real. Time passes but it does go somewhere. It was several centuries before this revolutionary understanding achieved its full cultural impact, but perhaps Augustine more than anyone else, and in spite of his formal Platonism, established the interest in history which characterizes Western culture. Augustine said: "Two loves built two cities, the earthly which is built up by the love of self to the contempt of God, and the heavenly which is built up by the love of God to the contempt of self."[6] Here he reflects Platonism and the sacred and profane loves of the *Symposium*, but he recognizes time as real, and hence he gives history a unidirectional thrust instead of the classic and Oriental rotation of souls. Time for Augustine is not the objective

[6] *De Civitate Dei*, XIV, xxviii.

movement of heavenly bodies either, as in ancient ho-
rology. Nor is it simply the movement of things in space,
as in modern science. Time is not to be found in things
at all. Time is in the soul, time is spiritual extension,
*distentio animae*. The past is the soul's remembrance,
the future is its expectation, and the present is its attention.

One might get the impression from Augustine that
time is the creation of the human soul. This would reduce all history to psychology, and at best we would end
in Platonic idealism. This would be a mistake, since
time is the *extension* of the human soul, not the invention. This means that time is a matter of the Spirit. Time
is the creation of God, or possibly it is the extension of
his life (*psyche*, soul). Insofar as man participates in the
life of God through the breath of the Spirit, he participates in God's time. The broken relation which is expressed in the Christian story by the fall means in terms
of time that this extension of God's life in us has been
broken, that our time is shattered so that its past is always dying to us and we slip away from it. But with
the restoration proleptically received in the resurrection, we begin to participate anew in the life and time
of God. This makes us co-creators of history. Our stewardship (*oikonomia*) in the economy of God is not just
keeping a trust for him, not just a guardian care of the
earth, but a creative, suffering share in the edification
and glorification of the entire creature. This is why the
unidirectional thrust in the progress of history has meaning.

What has this unidirectional thrust produced since its
inception in world history? We can only give a brief
suggestion of an answer. We have said that cultures develop from new visions of reality. The Christian dualism
expressed by Augustine, with its City of God and its
City of earth, its time of God and its broken historical

time, was a vision which radically affirms the reality of time in both God's City and man's. There have been variations on this theme, which describe the history of Christendom, but the basic dualism with the meaningful reality of time has never been shattered.

There have been great upheavals in history that may appear to some to be more radical than this shift in the view of time, but it would seem that, even apart from the faithful appreciation of the Christian story, the great division between B.C. and A.D. is still the most meaningful. Even the unbeliever will recognize that the vision of the reality of time has produced a culture in which historical movement has meaning, and that this radically distinguishes this culture from every other culture chronicled in the story of mankind.

It is popular among historians to point to 600 B.C. and 1500 A.D. as the two great thresholds of cultural change. They were great indeed, but not so great as the Christian vision of time, and there have been other thresholds just as significant. Certainly the Renaissance brought a tremendous modification of culture, but it was by no means as simple as it is often described, and it was really a modification rather than a radical change. The Renaissance was not simply the revival of humanism, in which everywhere men stopped looking to the heavens and started to seek human values. The social changes in this period were varied and not synchronized. A study of the succession of paintings from the unsigned triptychs of Medieval altars to the frescos of Giotto will show the gradual shift from abstract Medieval mystical and metaphysical idealism to Renaissance humanism. The figures of Giotto begin to have sorrowful eyes and pink, rounded cheeks instead of the flat faces and expressionless eyes of his nameless predecessors. The perspective of Mantegna and the classical themes of Botticelli increased this trend toward the human. But the human was idealized! The shift was not from the ideal to the natural. It was from the ideal metaphysical to the ideal human. This was true throughout the Italian Renaissance. Botticelli in Firenze and Titian in Venezia differed only in technique; their ideals were the same abstractions of human beauty, truth, and goodness.

But it was not the southern Renaissance that brought the greatest historical change. In the Flemish painters, beginning with Jan van Eyck, the shift was more radical. The Virgins and Christs of the northern painters are as ugly as peasants. Even the Christchild is painted wrinkled and red. While the Madonnas of the south are human in that the models were courtesans and princesses, they are nevertheless idealized. The shift in the north to the human was to the real and the natural. This more radical change in the north explains how the two regions got out of step in the Reformation, in the industrial revolution, and in political reform. While the south reverted to nonhistorical ideas, the north moved in the direction of positivism, materialism, and human realism. When the trend toward mysticism and divine aspiration attenuated Medieval culture, a new grasp of reality was required. The south returned to Platonism, but the north took the tack of historical materialism. Since this was more in accord with the thrust of reality, since human materialism has a more meaningful place for time than does human idealism, history was henceforth carried forward by northern European culture rather than by southern.

Regardless of these variegated upheavals, the original Christian dualism was retained. In Protestantism the dualism was no longer seen in terms of Augustine's two cities but was now defined in terms of a Visible World (including the state, the organized church, and all history) and the Invisible Church.

The Enlightenment retained the dualism too, only now all visible institutions — churches, states, societies —

were set up against the ideal of Reason. We have here a pendulum swing back to Plato again, and the realism of historical progress was neglected for the halcyon bliss of the Deists. But the period was short and the swing was not deep. Indeed because one of the ideals was freedom, the period was mixed with forces that in the nineteenth century quickly drew the movement sharply in the direction of a naive and uncritical optimism in evolutionary progress.

Karl Marx pushed the pendulum further in the same direction, though reversing the values from spiritual ideals to material reals. He found the basic dualism to be between the historical status quo with its *Überbau* of Christian and capitalist virtues and the economic determinism that would inevitably overthrow and bury the Christian-capitalist superstructure. There is much of both Jewish apocalypticism and German Rationalism in Marx, although these are inconsistent with each other. Yet it is significant that, far from opposing the Judeo-Christian view of the reality of time, this arch foe of Christianity made capital of it. The basic difference in his apocalyptic hope and messianic deliverance is, like that between Christianity and Judaism, only a difference in reading the timetable. Marx looks for deliverance as a historical thrust, but the sabbath rest of the stateless and classless society will come within history and will come by human revolutionary activity. It is interesting that both his eschatology and his morality are basically Christian, and still more important, his revolutionary methodology rests upon Christian historical realism.

It is evident, therefore, that from Tertullian to the present, with variations in the time of apocalyptic solution, a dualistic, conflict view of history has prevailed, together with a fundamental belief that the time of history is meaningfully real. There have been throwbacks in, for example, the static idealism of the Old

Liberals who found their inspiration in a romantic return to the tradition of the Greeks. There have been times of naive optimism, such as in the nineteenth century, when men put all their trust in a humanitarian moralism that was expected to work itself out in the evolutionary process of history. It is the collapse of this optimism and naturalism that has produced the chaotic condition in our culture today. But through all these changes, history itself is compellingly telling a story in which there is meaningful movement towards world community. Historical dramas from Shakespeare's plays on the kings of England to Osborne's *Luther,* and epic tales from Tolstoi's *War and Peace* to Michener's *Hawaii,* testify to the story quality of history. Stories do not take their character from history, history gets its meaning because it takes on the character of story.

Today meaning has broken down partly because men no longer believe in the absolutes of the Platonic system. This could be a relative skepticism in which merely the present forms in which the absolutes are cast have been called into question. If this is so, then new forms will soon be cast and the culture will proceed on the same first principles as before. Aldous Huxley has discussed the concept of history as the struggle for freedom against slavery in his novel *Eyeglass in Gaza.* The primal slavery is to the empty belly and the unpropitious season. This is slavery to nature, and men seek escape from nature through social organization and technical invention. In a modern city it is possible to forget that nature exists. But as soon as one slavery is abolished, the new freedom produces an institution which inflicts a new slavery. When nature is abolished, religious, legal, military, economic, educational, artistic, and scientific institutions are erected which provide meaning for the work of man. Every time a revolt is made against the encrustation of an institution, there is anarchy, an intolerable reversion to the slavery of nature. To escape this atavistic slavery, new forms are given to the institutions civilized men have invented. For a time there is a honeymoon of freedom, but soon these forms ossify and men are again broken by them.

The breakdown of the Platonic system may be more radical, however, in which case it will not be a matter of changing social forms but of supplying new institutions. There is serious doubt today that there is ultimacy of goodness, truth, beauty, even reality itself. There is further doubt in the eschatological victory of the historical movement. It would be a grave mistake, however, to view the breakdown of the Platonic system of meaning as the breakdown of religion, especially of Christianity. The Christian message does not rest upon the absolutes of idealism. The faith of Christians that God will prevail over the rebellious usurpation of the evil One is not the same as the rational conviction that the Absolute is good. But the Christian does trust in the ultimate goodness of God's story. He hopes in a blessed deliverance from the sickness unto death. If this too is being doubted today, we have a despair which challenges directly the Christian faith.

Much of the challenge is, to be sure, directed against the forms of Christian institutions. Where these forms are outdated and incapable of functioning for the purpose for which they were created, they should be abolished. We see the organized church attacked today more because it is laughably ineffectual than because it is a threat to somebody's freedom. The pastor in Ibsen's *Ghosts* is portrayed with satirical invective because he is the symbol of a power structure that compromised morality. The rector in Tennessee Williams' *Cat on a Hot Tin Roof*, however, is dismissed comically with only a few lines. In one he asks for the bathroom. In another he is called in at the critical moment when Big Daddy

is to be told he is dying of cancer. It seems the proper
time to have the symbol of religion say the right word,
but the rector can only mumble: "I think I had better
go home now."

We should welcome the critical slices of the literary
sword. They cut away rotten wood. But the quest for a
timeless solution to the decaying elements of temporal
institutions is a wrong approach. It is equally wrong to
look for secular forms to help us revitalize the church.
We hear it said that the church must be relevant to the
age, and no one can dispute this, but then we are quickly tempted to examine our religious forms and take those
forms which seem best to conform with the intellectual
and political climate of our day. We find that currently
men reject absolutes, and so we try to define the faith
in terms of the relativity that is so popular. Since among
the existentialists the essence of being is denied in favor
of the concretion of existence, theology and christology
become reduced to existential anthropology. Notions of
a pre-existent Christ and a post-resurrection reality are
revised in the direction of an adoptionist christology and
a resurrection of the message, or the community, or the
idea of freedom. These are solutions offered by scholars
like Bultmann and van Buren, much in the tradition of
such earlier interpreters as Schleiermacher, who tried to
make Christianity acceptable to its cultured despisers.

In the present crisis Christopher Dawson says we
should look rather to those social forms which best conform to religious men. Instead of trying to make Christian doctrines and Christian practices fit into the forms
which secular society already accepts, we should look at
the political, economic, and aesthetic forms to see what
is genuinely Christian in them. This would support our
thesis that religious consciousness carries a culture forward and gives it meaning. In every secular form there
is both a genuine and a fraudulent religious content.

Hidden beneath the fraud or disguised on the surface, somewhere in every form, there is the mark of God and his Christ. We must discover it and bring it to the careful attention of religious men, that is, men who have also the mark of God and his Christ. The struggle for open housing, for example, has genuine Christian content. Here old economic and political forms must be changed, and the change will appeal to men of good will. The struggle for peace through conflict provides a story that is rich in meaning.

If history can be told as story, then stories can be told as history. This has been done with remarkable ingenuity and enchanting originality by J. R. R. Tolkien. Perhaps no literature, apart from the Bible, demonstrates the meaning of story for history better than the completely fanciful history of Middle-earth. Tolkien's books include *The Hobbit,* the three volumes of *The Lord of the Rings,* and several shorter tales and poems, all of which concern a host of imaginary creatures in the fabled realm of Middle-earth. By sheer invention Tolkien has created a story that has its own history covering four ages, the first going back into the dim recesses of unrecorded past, but the third being the great age of struggle for the mysterious Ring of Power. The fourth age ushers in the dominion of Men, when Elves and Dwarves and other creatures of faerie diminish and slip into the silence and shadow of unbelief. The story has its own geography too, with great regions stretching in all directions, some well cultivated and others as yet unexplored wilderness. Tolkien has even invented a language, or a family of languages, with a linguistic history deriving from ancient Elvish. There is also a Common Speech, Westrom, spoken and understood by the various creatures from different regions. The heroes of Tolkien's tale are Hobbits, strange, furry-footed little people who live comfortably in a Shire. They have their family lineage, as do men, and they enter into the mortality of men. One of their number, Frodo, was chosen to destroy a magic ring, the Ring of Power, by returning it to the fires of Mount Doom, where it was forged under the wicked reign of Sauron the Dark Lord. Frodo's adventures carry him into strange places where Elves and Dwarves and talking trees dwell, where men engage in great wars over the kingdoms of Middle-earth, where Wizards and Ringwraiths battle for supremacy and little people are caught in the mystery of a cosmic struggle that has skirmishes on the surface of history but deeper wars at the core of reality.

Tolkien's story is the epic tale of good conquering evil, but the victory is not absolute because it is bought at an enormous price. The Ring is the symbol of power. Power is sought by everyone. Its quest is apparently the meaning of life. All creatures think that possessing it will bring satisfaction, that losing it will bring poverty, weakness, degradation, and defeat. There is One Ring for the Dark Lord, that which gives power to rule over all and ironically which binds in darkness everyone who seeks its power. Either we have the wisdom and courage to destroy our Ring of Power, or we are destroyed by it. This is the meaning of the history of the Hobbits in Tolkien's fabulous tale.

Reality is thus seen to be an adventure in the use of power. Freedom is a possibility for all creatures, but progress toward love and holiness, peace and justice, within the bounds of freedom is precarious and beset with troubles. Yet we must not flinch at even the direst disasters. As Zorba the Greek said, "Life *is* trouble; only death is not." Bitter conflict with mysterious evil is written into the story of all history in every age as well as into the personal history of every creature. Meaning is to be found not by escape into a mystic void nor in a nihilistic revolt. And if we can accept neither the intellectual idealism of a timeless absolute nor the sentimental and wishful projection of meaning into an apocalyptic future, then we must find meaning in a real temporal story that includes both conflict and victory, sacrifice and satisfaction, suspense and resolution, mystery and integrity. Life is trouble, but the trouble has excitement and the adventure has meaning because we are committed to go somewhere. It is true that we do not know the precise place and character of our destination, but we do know the right way and we know it is worth taking the journey. And on our way we also know two other things. We know the pangs of separation and death in which we cry out with Jesus on his cross: "My God, my God, why hast thou forsaken me?" And we know the certainty of his resurrection victory since we share it with him in the communion of his church, and therefore we can also say with him while still on that same cross, "Father, into thy hands I commit my spirit."

# VI

## Conclusion:
## The Meaning of the Christian Story

We have made a voyage of discovery in the realm of story. Our discussion does not pretend to be exhaustive, nor even systematic. Partly this sketchy treatment is due to the experimental nature of this initial sortie, partly it is due to the nature of story itself. In addition to the rich insights stories give as reflections of our times, we have found that story itself, seen as a category, gives us a clue to the nature of reality. From among the many treasures buried in story, we have taken five jewels and given them somewhat careful examination. Thus we have found that reality is the story of the anguished and the possessed. The universe is in rebellion and under a spell. The ambiguity of evil is not illusory. The struggle is real, and everyone is caught in it from the tiniest twig to the Lord Almighty. There is in the midst of evil an irrepressible looking for love, but love is a many-faceted gem, and some of the facets reflect the ugliness of lust while others shine with the beauty of sacrifice. Reality will not rest until it reaches a holiness that is healthy and whole, that is awesomely different from the sickness unto death that is familiar to this world. But since this love and holiness cannot be achieved, there is abiding in the breast of everyman a hope and a dream of deliv-

erance beyond the scope of history. The final meaning
of life is seen, therefore, to be an adventure in which
freedom and power are the goals, and love and holiness
come in the search not as rewards for merit, but as gifts
to help us achieve a creative balance in the use of freedom and power.

We have looked briefly into history and seen it to be
a chapter in the greater story of reality. We have now,
finally, to ask what is the full meaning of the Christian
story itself. We shall attempt to answer this in a token
way by directing our attention to what the Christian
story must necessarily mean to practical behavior as men
find themselves acting out their roles as the story of
reality proceeds. The pragmatic concern is necessary
because the economy of God, the divine stewardship,
is precisely what is at work in the life of the creature
at the core of reality. As Paul said to the Ephesians:
"For we are his workmanship, created in Christ Jesus
for good works, which God prepared beforehand, that
we should walk in them" (Eph. 2:10). And also to the
Philippians: "For God is at work in you, both to will
and to work for his good pleasure" (Phil. 2:13).

The coming of Jesus has revealed, like sight to the
blind, a new understanding of life, history, and all
reality. We can see ourselves in the movement of an
exciting drama, the climax of which occurs in the third
act. Most of the scenes in all three acts are still, for us,
played out in the sequence of history, but we now know
that the drama stretches far beyond. There is a crucial
point, however, where history and the full story coin-
cide. At this point in the story of salvation, the identity
of two characters is disclosed, characters who have been
acting in a mysterious way from the beginning but who
have been hidden behind strange masks. The Word of
God has been speaking from the flies and the Spirit of
the Lord has been giving life from the wings, and be-

cause of this dual action and passion of divine power, all creatures have come into being and have moved toward their eternal destiny. But now with the historical incidence of Jesus, the Holy Spirit and Christ have become manifest to the elect family of God in a way which radically changes this destiny.

In the first act of the drama of salvation God is found extremely close to the processes of nature. The great pagan religions recognized this with their devotion to fertility and the natural cycle of birth and death. All of life, labor, and leisure found meaning that was expressed through periodic communal festivals of thanksgiving for nature's gifts. Progress and change is abhorrent at this level because there is no thought of an eternal destiny with a real goal in the future. Everything is caught in the cycle of nature, which constantly repeats itself. Practical behavior and morality become a simple matter of dividing a pie. Ethics in such a view rests on the principle of rights in which each man is an island protected by the rule of *suum cuique*. So long as everyone respects what belongs to everybody else, justice and peace will be established. And to insure the perpetuation of the system, a token offering is brought to the gods with an attitude of appeasement at the least and gratitude at the highest. There is as yet no real understanding of the story character of life, history, or reality.

This pious awareness of nature's gifts and of the need for dividing an offering in recognition of the divine source has sustained men in various civilizations for centuries. It was their dim vision of reality that built the kind of culture that lived on the cycle of nature. High religions and profound philosophies have been erected around it from the time of the ancient Indians and Greeks to the present. In modern times some philosophers, like Bergson, Whitehead, and Teilhard de Chardin, have refreshingly reminded us of the closeness of

God to the processes of nature, and in addition they have tried to break out of the static cycle of the ancient immanental view by pointing to a unidirectional process that is proclaimed by the eschatological thrust of the Christian message. For them God is the concrescence of emergent novelty in the creative passage. From this point of view there is no sharp distinction between nature and grace. Indeed grace is conceived as a movement of spirit attending not only the redemptive aspects of humanity, but also with depth and spontaneity attending the whole of created realities.

While this philosophy has its appealing depth, it still belongs in the first act of the drama. Both the recognition of the closeness of God to nature and the insight of a unidirectional thrust in the process of reality are salutary, but between nature and grace there is a difference that is acknowledged only when the uniqueness of story is fully comprehended. To speak of God's creative care of the universe as grace is to generalize to the exclusion of his unique dramatic deliverance of the creature from its bondage to death.

The currently more prestigious philosophy of Paul Tillich even more obviously finds its lines in this first act because of his essentially immanental metaphysics. With his concept of the Ground of Being, Tillich holds fast to the more static categories of Plato, in contrast to the process philosophy of Whitehead and Teilhard, with its place for emergent novelty. As the distinction between the sacred and the secular is wiped out, so the dichotomy between nature and supernature is disallowed. With God as the Ground of Being, rather than the Supreme Being who stands above us, there is an ontological continuity running through all reality. This makes the notion of a divine being coming in the flesh of humanity absurd. The incarnation, which is the climactic event in the third act of the Christian story, is therefore not appreciated by Tillich; instead he prefers to look upon Jesus as the example of one who achieved perfect God-consciousness. The result of this tradition in theological thinking, all of which is rooted in Schleiermacher, is that a piety of personal stewardship is defined which is limited to a grateful response to nature's gifts. There is no possibility of seeing nature itself, and man, and all history, as active and passionate participants in a grand and moving story. There is only, in Tillich's view, the hope for serenity in the eternal Now, a view which compared to the admittedly ambiguous and suspenseful adventure of story must be judged as insufferably boring.

That the story has moved on, however, is demonstrated by a simple observation of the world about us. Man's prowess over nature has changed his life so radically that he no longer sees nature as the giver of his sustenance. Now nature has become only the repository of materials for his artifacts. If man is to be grateful for the real thing in his life, he must be grateful for the intelligence he uses in the manufacture of his materials. He lives now, not by the whim of nature for which he formerly shaped his piety as joyful gratitude, but by his inventive genius in manipulating nature. Man limited to a God of natural process or to the Ground of Being is therefore in danger of losing all piety whatever. Being grateful to oneself is scarcely a pattern of piety, especially when this same intelligent self may through fearful miscalculation or defiant greed obliterate all life on this planet.

It is at this point that the revelation of God in the Bible speaks most clearly, calling us out of the natural piety of simple gratitude into a covenant piety in which our stewardship is directed responsibly to our fellows in the community. Perhaps this is the profound significance of the story of Cain and Abel, in which Cain failed to learn the painful lesson that he was his brother's keeper, that the right division of his offering included care for others. The stewardship of gratitude for nature's gifts is now replaced by the stewardship of obligation to one's neighbor. Here the second act in the drama of salvation is played, with God's covenant with Israel providing the lines of the Torah for the role of human behavior. Now we see God as a person who speaks to his creatures. He is not embedded in the process of the being of our reality. He stands over against us in free address. We live by the utterance of his speech and the breath of his Spirit, but since he has made us in his image, he never violates our freedom. It is this freedom in which we are addressed as persons which turns simple gratitude into a sense of obligation. When we are obliged to come together, we form communities with law, and as a result history is set on its course. The law given to Moses was not the only law that produced a community. There are many similar stories because there is a common legality in every culture. The distinctive aspect of the Mosaic covenant is that although it was divinely given, it was provisional and proleptic. Unlike all those legal codes that have claimed absolute sanction, the Mosaic covenant was given only as a temporary expedient until a prior promise could be fulfilled.

The ethics of covenant piety rests on the principle of obligation in which all men are brothers in the family chosen by God. So long as every member of the family respects his obligation to every other member, the family will prosper under the promise of God. "Blessed is the man who walks not in the counsel of the wicked. . . . He is like a tree planted by streams of water, that yields its fruit in its season, and its leaf does not wither. In all that he does, he prospers" (Ps. 1:1-3). Destiny in the chosen family in history is determined by the faithfulness with which one keeps the covenant. This is no longer a matter of seasonal appeasement or occasional gratitude; this is now ultimate destiny, which therefore shapes every moment before God.

But God's revelation does not stop with nature and history. He has come to us in the *uniform* behavior of the natural process and taught us to be grateful. He has come to us in the *unidirectional* thrust of history and taught us to be responsible. But he has also come to us in a third act in the *unique* disclosure of his Son and taught us to be creative as we share his new life in the resurrection community. It is not enough that we recognize our responsible stewardship in the management of the resources God has given us. We must also accept the challenge of the creative development of these resources. We are not only to name and distribute various creatures under our dominion; we are not only to cut up a pie equitably. We must also create and produce new things in a burgeoning, ballooning economy under the direction of the Spirit. We do not neglect gratitude and obligation as we move into the third act of our story, but as we come into the creative life of the Spirit we change our fearful appeasement and legal justice into joyful thanksgiving and spontaneous responsibility.

Man has been trying in his checkered career to tame the wilderness and harness nature. He has been trying to bring order out of the irrational forces of nature and establish a society. We are rapidly coming to the point where we no longer have nature as our environment, as the thing existing around us which we work. We have instead as our immediate environment the society we have ordered. Whereas before we had things that could be used for our needs, we now have people who need to be managed. By manipulating people in the organization of our work, we make them things. Instead of loving people and using things, we find ourselves loving things and using people. As Augustine said, we use what we should enjoy and we enjoy what we should use, and this is the core of sin.

In the resurrection community in which Christians live in the presence of the risen Lord and by the guidance of the Holy Spirit, there is no fixed code of moral absolutes. There is no blueprint for utopia. There are no laws we can know beforehand which will tell us what to do in a given situation. This is because we no longer live as impersonal parts of a natural process nor as cases in a legally constituted community. Our destiny goes beyond nature and history as persons who freely participate in the creative thrust of the Spirit. We live and walk and work by the Spirit, and therefore we must strive to find a meaningful place for all persons in this new community. Each is given his role, but the precise lines that he speaks are not given — he must contribute freely and creatively to the story.

The pressing problem of the modern world is to keep the machine age from dehumanizing and depersonalizing people. It is only the fact of the Spirit working in our midst that guarantees both the freedom to be persons and the reverence of personal concern for everything in the cosmos, great and small. The unique and surprising development in the drama of salvation is the coming of the Spirit. This is what makes us Christians, for it is by the Spirit that we recognize Jesus to be Lord and by the Spirit that we pray to the Father. And it is by the Creator-Spirit that we move forward in our destiny, transcending ourselves in a creative thrust as participants with God himself as we pass together from glory to glory. "Now the Lord is the Spirit, and where the Spirit of the Lord is, there is freedom. And we all, with unveiled face, beholding the glory of the Lord, are being changed into his likeness from one degree of glory to another; for this comes from the Lord who is the Spirit" (II Cor. 3:17-18).

The work of the Spirit in our practical behavior is to bring men above the natural process and out of the historical community of law into a creative, personal community of resurrection. Here the religious life means that we do not exploit nature and simply give God thanks for it, nor do we organize men only with justice and say we are obliged, but rather we wait upon the Spirit and jump with joy at his spontaneous direction, for he will lead us into freedom and power.

Roth, Robert

Story and reality

# DATE DUE

| 12-14-01 | | | |
|---|---|---|---|
| | | | |
| | | | |
| | | | |
| | | | |
| | | | |
| | | | |
| | | | |
| | | | |
| | | | |
| | | | |
| | | | |
| | | | |
| | | | |
| | | | |
| | | | |
| | | | |
| | | | |